笃行汉语·课外读物系列

周敏 著

学汉字So Easy:
中英双语图说汉字

中国·广州

图书在版编目（CIP）数据

学汉字 So Easy：中英双语图说汉字/ 周敏著．—广州：暨南大学出版社，2014.3
（笃行汉语·课外读物系列）
ISBN 978－7－5668－0667－3

Ⅰ.①学…　Ⅱ.①周…　Ⅲ.①汉字—对外汉语教学—教材　Ⅳ.①H195.4

中国版本图书馆 CIP 数据核字（2013）第 162246 号

出版发行：暨南大学出版社

地　址：中国广州暨南大学
电　话：总编室（8620）85221601
　　　　营销部（8620）85225284　85228291　85228292（邮购）
传　真：（8620）85221583（办公室）　85223774（营销部）
邮　编：510630
网　址：http：//www.jnupress.com　http：//press.jnu.edu.cn

排　版：弓设计
印　刷：佛山市浩文彩色印刷有限公司

开　本：787mm×960mm　1/16
印　张：12.875
字　数：252 千
版　次：2014 年 3 月第 1 版
印　次：2014 年 3 月第 1 次

定　价：29.80 元

总 序

“笃行”一词见于《礼记·中庸》：“博学之，审问之，慎思之，明辨之，笃行之。”作为治学或者学习活动的最后一个阶段，“笃行”意味着只有知识付诸实践才是一次学习活动的真正完成，也只有能够付诸实践的知识才是真正的知识。本书系命名为“笃行汉语”，兼有上述两种意思。

就作为第二语言的汉语教学而言，它的直接目的是学生汉语综合能力的养成和提高。服务于这个目标，我们一方面重视教材、教法的实践性，另一方面也充分认识到，在学习活动中，知识内化为能力和自觉的意识是一个复杂的、多重因素共同作用的过程。而且，越是到高级阶段，所需仰赖的纯语言学意义的知识的比例便越小。因此，本书系拟分为两大类四个系列。其中，语言技能系列、专业汉语系列旨在培养学生的基本汉语技能以及在某一领域（譬如商务活动、酒店旅游、汉语教学等）内运用汉语的能力；文学文化系列、课外读物系列主要针对中高级汉语程度的学生，强化其在跨文化交际活动中以文化行事的能力。就后一大类而言，它和坊间同类书籍的最大区别在于，它尤为重视培养学生的文化能力或以文化行事的能力，而不是单纯的知识学习、文化体验。

“忠信笃敬”是暨南大学所恪守的校训，“笃行”之意包含于其中；“忠信笃敬、知行合一、自强不息、和而不同”的暨南精神，更说明了暨南人对科学的实践精神的自觉承担。华文学院是暨南大学面向海外及港、澳、台地区开展华文教育、对外汉语教学和预科教育的国际化专门学院。学院师资力量雄厚，人才培养体系完善，学习条件优越，生活环境舒适。半个世纪以来，华文学院共培养了十万余名学子，遍及全球五大洲，桃李满天下。目前，华文学院已经成为位于中国南方的，集科学研究、教材研发、人才培养、师资培训于一体，在国内外享有盛誉的华文教育及对外汉语教学重镇，每年都有来自全球几十个国家和地区的数千名学生入读华文学院。2012 年，暨南大学华文教育研究院成立，标志着华文学院的发展跨上了新的台阶。目前，华文教育研究院正在研发的华文水平测试、华文教师资格认证，以及各国别华文本土化教材的编写，都将为世界华文教育事业、汉语国际推广事业作出重要贡献。

笃行汉语书系以华文学院强大的师资力量、完善的课程体系和丰厚的教学实践经验为依托，所收入的教材都是编写者在自身所承担课程的多轮讲授过程中积累、酝酿而出的。可以说，它出自经验丰富、学养深厚的一线教师之手，是华文学院汉语教学类课程建设的有机组成，具有极强的实战性、针对性，因此也必将对汉语学习者语言能力的提高有所助益。

暨南大学出版社是国务院侨务办公室主管、暨南大学主办的综合性大学出版社，多年来坚持“为教学科研服务，为侨务工作服务”的出版宗旨，尤其注重华文教育和传统文化类图书的开发，其中由暨南大学华文学院主编的《中文》和由北京华文学院主编的《汉语》教材全球发行量已超一千万册，是海外发行量最大的华文教材，受到海内外华文学习者的广泛赞誉。笃行汉语书系是华文学院与暨南大学出版社的又一次合作。我们相信，在双方的共同努力下，笃行汉语书系一定能够坚定地、持续地走下去，走出属于自己的一片天地！

笃行汉语书系编委会

2013 年 5 月于暨南园

序

有人说：完成一部著作，就像生下一个孩子。今天我说：周敏完成这本《学汉字 so easy》，我就像外婆得了一个外孙女！在揉进了被升级换代带来的几丝落寞情感中，更多的是生生不息所带来的兴奋与喜悦。

学汉字 so easy，但撰写这本书却不 easy。孕育小孩是怀胎十月，而这本小书是怀胎四年。自周敏 2009 年入读深圳大学文学院硕士研究生，我们师生俩就商讨出这一选题。周敏本科为英语专业，硕士为汉语言文字学专业，我觉得这一选题能够将她这两个专业的优势最大化地“扬长”。写作过程中，周敏付出几多汗水，几多艰辛，一一历历在我目。“数易其稿”尚不足以言其认真严谨，而是“数十易其稿”。记得一次，我约见周敏讨论该书的写作，也怪我催得急，她跑步而来，呼吸急促、面色苍白，大汗淋漓，苗条清丽的身体几近晕倒。原来是因为赶写此书，她身体透支，已经好些天没好好吃饭休息了！

《学汉字 so easy》，相信会有不少读者喜欢。假如你是会英文的朋友，她能帮助你学习汉字汉语；假如你是会中文的朋友，她不仅能帮助你进一步了解汉字汉语，还能帮助你学习英文。汉字是世界上最具特色的、唯一现存的自源文字，配上图画及古字字形，直观有趣，解说重点突出，简明晓畅，易懂易学。所附录的《附录：编写说明》，从理论的高度，较深入地说明了由选题选字选词、到解字解词的理据及原则，可以帮助我们更好地理解本书内容。

在“外婆”的眼中，《学汉字 so easy》，中英混血独具风采，是个小清新、小可爱的“外孙女”。读者朋友们，您怎么看?

曹兆兰

2013 年 4 月

前言

人类文明史上起源最早的文字，目前公认的有两河流域的苏美尔楔形文字、尼罗河流域的埃及圣体文、中国的汉字和中美洲的玛雅文字。楔形文字和圣体文早在两千多年前就已经消亡，直到18世纪才被破解。虽然中美洲的玛雅印第安人仍能说玛雅语，但其文字早在16世纪就成为死文字。目前，只有中国的汉字是唯一连续使用三千多年并且仍然在使用的文字。

随着中国经济的发展和影响力的增强，越来越多的外国友人加入到了学习汉语、了解中国文化的队伍中。在对外汉语教学中，对外汉字教学一直是重点，但同时也是难点。外国人的汉字认读和书写能力，直接影响到他们对汉语的掌握。

在20世纪90年代前期，汉字教学一直附属于汉语教学，而相应的汉字教材也少且不精。到了90年代后期，随着对外汉字教学研究的深入开展，这种现象才有所改观，并出版了一批对外汉字教材。但同时我也发现，目前还没有一本将古文字知识、现代汉语知识以及英语结合起来的汉字教材。那么，编写这样一本教材就非常有必要了。

首先，本书选择了800个甲级字中的148个独体字作为编写对象。《汉语水平词汇与汉字等级大纲》中的“等级汉字”涵盖了留学生学习及考试用到的绝大部分汉字，是对外汉语汉字教学的主要依据。其中，又以字频及所对应的词汇分级为基础，将2 905个汉字分为甲、乙、丙、丁四级。甲级字是其中字频最高、对应词汇最多的字，而独体字又是甲级字中最简单易学且最有生成能力的字。

其次，汉字具有“书画同源”的特点，每一个汉字都是一幅图画，都有一个故事。因此，本书给每个字配上了图片，列出了古文字字形，讲解了字源。这样不仅增强了趣味性和直观性，展示了汉字演变的过程，还能让学习者在学习汉字的同时深入了解中国传统文化。

再次，本书给每个字配上相对应的甲级、乙级词汇，使得学习者在学习汉字的同时掌握每个汉字的表达功能。同时列出以某字表示意义或读音的一系列字，以增强学习者对汉字结构特点的认识，扩展学习内容。

最后，给整张识字卡配上英文翻译，以方便非汉字文化圈初学者学习。

本书从最初构思到最后成文，我的导师曹兆兰教授付出了巨大心血。本书从构思阶段到写作过程都得到了曹老师的悉心指导，书稿完成后，曹老师还做了大量的校对、审核工作，甚至为本书联系出版单位，可以说没有曹老师的帮助就不会有这本小书。本书还得到了汕头大学潘家懿教授的指导和帮助，同时也承蒙暨南大学出版社的杜小陆编辑给予支持。在此，谨向各位老师、前辈和朋友表示衷心感谢。

由于作者学识浅薄、水平有限，书中错误及不妥之处在所难免，敬请对外汉语教学的专家学者和师友批评指正。

周　敏

2013 年于深圳

目 录

148 字音序检索表

148 字分类检索表

人体

动物

非 fēi …… 25
飞 fēi …… 24
合 hé …… 36
角 jiǎo …… 48
马 mǎ …… 63
毛 máo …… 64
牛 niú …… 73
求 qiú …… 84
肉 ròu …… 87
西 xī …… 113
羊 yáng …… 123
也 yě …… 124
鱼 yú …… 134
为 wéi/wèi …… 108
半 bàn …… 4

植物

本 běn …… 5
才 cái …… 8
干 gān/gàn …… 29
来 lái …… 56
米 mǐ …… 67
亲 qīn …… 83
世 shì …… 98
束 shù …… 102
不 bù …… 7
丰 fēng …… 26
个 gè …… 30
果 guǒ …… 35
齐 qí …… 78
生 shēng …… 94

自然

日 rì …… 86
电 diàn …… 17
回 huí …… 41
火 huǒ …… 43
气 qì …… 80
山 shān …… 89
水 shuǐ …… 103
雨 yǔ …… 135
月 yuè …… 137
云 yún …… 139

人造物

厂 chǎng …… 10
车 chē …… 11
单 dān …… 14
刀 dāo …… 15
东 dōng …… 18
方 fāng …… 23
工 gōng …… 31
公 gōng …… 32
黑 hēi …… 37
互 hù …… 38
户 hù …… 39
会 huì …… 42
己 jǐ …… 45
斤 jīn …… 50
乐 yuè/lè …… 138
力 lì …… 59
两 liǎng …… 61
门 mén …… 66
南 nán …… 72

数字

识字卡

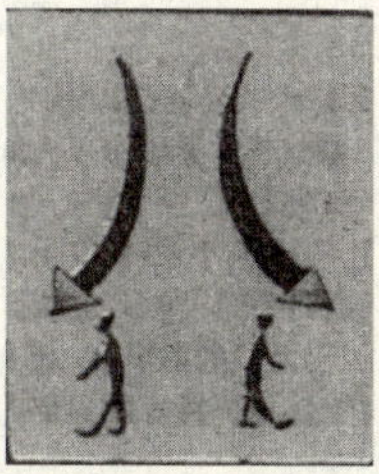

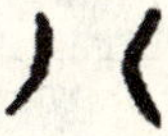			八 bā
甲骨文 Oracle bone script	金文 Bronze inscriptions	小篆 Small seal script	楷书 Regular script

“八”，甲骨文和金文字形相同，左右两笔向背而画，所以“八”有“扒开”、“分开”等意义。用作数词“八”是记音。

In the etymological sense，“八” means to push aside or separate. It is made up of two opposite strokes，forming a symmetrical symbol “八”. Now people use it to indicate eight.

丿 八

四面八方 sìmiànbāfāng from far and near	乱七八糟 luànqībāzāo be in a muddle or a mess 七嘴八舌 qīzuǐbāshé everybody talking at the same time
以八为意符的字 Characters with “八” to signify meaning	意符在上：分 公
小提示 Tips	“八”在书写时，先写撇，再写捺，撇和捺相离。第一笔撇写得稍微长一点，我们把它称为长撇。 The left-falling long stroke of “八” is written before the right-falling one.

				白 bái
	甲骨文 Oracle bone script	金文 Bronze inscriptions	小篆 Small seal script	楷书 Regular script
	“白”，甲骨文和金文中，象人的拇指之形，后来指白色是记音。小篆上面加了短竖，楷书将短竖改为一撇，成为现代汉字字形。 The written form of “白” on oracle bone and bronze is like a thumb. Originally it means “thumb”, then is used to mean “white”.			丿 亻 白 白 白

白菜 báicài 白天 báitiān	Chinese cabbage daytime	我喜欢吃白菜。 Wǒ xǐhuān chī báicài. I like eating Chinese cabbage. 你白天在干什么？ Nǐ báitiān zài gàn shénme? What do you do during daytime?

小提示 Tips	“白”单独书写时，扁而宽；“白”作为“怕”和“拍”的偏旁书写时，狭而长。 When “白” is written separately, it should be a bit wider. While as the radical of “怕” and “拍”, it should be narrower.

				百 bǎi
	甲骨文 Oracle bone script	金文 Bronze inscriptions	小篆 Small seal script	楷书 Regular script
	“百”，甲骨文和金文均由两部分组成，下部是“白”，象人的拇指之形，上部加指事符号“一”，与“白”相区别，表示数字“一百”。 The earliest form of “百” is made up of “白” and a horizontal “一”, which is used to distinguish “百” from “白”. “百” originally means one hundred.			

老百姓 lǎobǎixìng	common people	中国老百姓现在过着幸福的生活。 Zhōngguó lǎobǎixìng xiànzài guòzhe xìngfú de shēnghuó. Populace in China live a very happy life now.

小提示 Tips	“白”字上面加一横就是“百”。 “百” can be composed by adding a horizontal stroke to the top of “白”.

		半 bàn
金文 Bronze inscriptions	小篆 Small seal script	楷书 Regular script

"半"，金文和小篆中，上部是"八"，表示从中间分开；下部是"牛"。上下两部分合起来表示：把一头牛分成两半，"半"从而有了"分半"、"一半"之义。

The earliest form of "半" is an ideograph drawn from "八" and "牛". The upper part "八" indicates dividing something into two, and the lower portion represents a bull. The two components put together to mean dividing the bull into two. Therefore, "半" has the meanings "to part something in the middle" and "half".

丶 丷 䒑 兰 半

半天	bàntiān	half of the day	半拉	bànlǎ	half
			半夜	bànyè	midnight
			一半	yībàn	half
			半导体	bàndǎotǐ	semiconductor

小提示 Tips

除了表示时间或实物的一半，"半"还可以表示空间的一半，例如"半路上"、"半山腰"等。

Besides expressing half of time or object, "半" also could indicate half of space, for example, "半路上" and "半山腰".

金文 Bronze inscriptions	小篆 Small seal script	楷书 Regular script
		本 běn

"本"，金文和小篆中，字形像一棵树。金文下部的一点、小篆下部的一横，起指事作用，指树的根部，所以"本"的本义指"树根"。因树根是树生长的基础，后"本"引申为"基础"、"本质"等意义。

The ancient form of "本" is an ideograph drawn from a tree and a dot (later a horizontal), which indicates the roots of the tree. So originally it means "the roots of a tree". As root is the base of a tree, "本" is extended to mean "foundation" or "essence".

一 十 才 木 本

本子	běnzi	notebook
基本	jīběn	basis
课本	kèběn	textbook
本来	běnlái	at first
本领	běnlǐng	capability
本事	běnshì	ability
本质	běnzhì	essence
根本	gēnběn	root/foundation

小提示
Tips

"木"的上面加一横成为"末"，表示树的末梢；"木"的下面加一横成为"本"，表示树的根部。

"末", written by adding a horizontal on the top of "木", means the end of a tree branch; "本", written by adding a horizontal on the bottom of "木", means the roots of a tree.

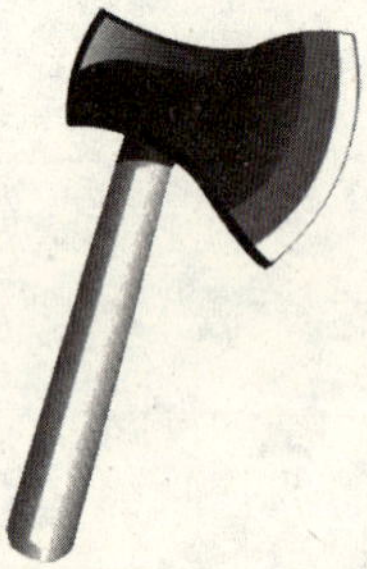

金文 1 Bronze inscriptions 1	金文 2 Bronze inscriptions 2	小篆 Small seal script	楷书 Regular script
	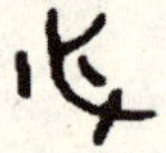		必 bì

"必"，金文字形中，上部的缺口处用于捆绑斧头，下部是弯曲的斧柄，左右两点指用于固定斧头的穿孔，所以"必"引申为"必定"之义。

The ancient form of "必" is a stand, which is used to bind axe. The lower part is the shaft, and the two dots on right and left are the holes used to fix the axe. Therefore, "必" is extended to mean "be bound to".

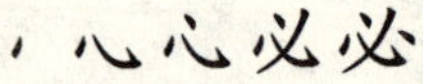

必须	bìxū	must/have to	必然	bìrán	inevitable
			必要	bìyào	necessary
			不必	bùbì	need not/not have to

小提示 Tips

"心"字加一撇就是"必"；"必"字先写第四笔撇，再写末笔的一点。

The character "必" is written by adding a left-falling stroke on "心" and the left-falling stroke is written before the final dot.

甲骨文 Oracle bone script	金文 Bronze inscriptions	小篆 Small seal script	楷书 Regular script
			不 bù

"不"，甲骨文、金文及小篆字形相近，象花的萼足之形，本义指"花萼"。因为其音与否定副词的音相同，所以后来"不"这个字形就用作否定副词，指"不是"或"没有"，而本义逐渐不再使用。

The ancient form of "不" is a pictograph of a calyx, therefore it originally means "calyx". Later "不" is used as a negative adverb to express "no" or "not", and its original meaning is disused.

一 丆 不 不

不错	bùcuò	correct/not bad
不要	bùyào	don't
不但	bùdàn	not only
不用	bùyòng	need not
不久	bùjiǔ	before long
不如	bùrú	not as good as
不同	bùtóng	different
对不起	duìbùqǐ	sorry/forgive me
不必	bùbì	need not
不论	bùlùn	no matter
不然	bùrán	or else
不断	bùduàn	continuous/continual/continually
不管	bùguǎn	no matter/regardless of
不过	bùguò	but
不许	bùxǔ	not allow
不仅	bùjǐn	not only
不少	bùshǎo	not a few/quite a few
不行	bùxíng	won't do

小提示 Tips

在现代汉语中，"不"通常用作否定副词。

In modern Chinese, "不" is usually used as a negative adverb to express "no" or "not".

甲骨文 Oracle bone script	金文 Bronze inscriptions	小篆 Small seal script	才 cái 楷书 Regular script

"才"，甲骨文和金文中，像草木刚刚破土而出的样子，上部的一横代表地面，一竖则代表长出地面的草木。所以"才"本义指"刚生长出来的草木"，又由此引申出"刚刚"、"方才"等意思。

The earliest form of "才" relates to ground, which is represented by the horizontal. The vertical indicates grass or a tree, which just break through the soil. Therefore, "才" originally means "trees and grass that just break through soil". By extension, it means "just now".

一 十 才

刚才 gāngcái just now/a moment ago	人才 réncái talented person

小提示 Tips	要注意区别"才"与"寸"，"才"的第三笔是一撇，"寸"是一点。 Be aware of the difference between the left-falling stroke in "才" and the dot in "寸".

				長	长 cháng zhǎng
	甲骨文 Oracle bone script	金文 Bronze inscriptions	小篆 Small seal script	楷书（繁体） Regular script (complex form)	楷书（简体） Regular script (simplified form)

"长"，甲骨文和金文中，字形像披着长发的人，特别突出了长长的头发。先民有蓄长发的习惯，故头发越长，年龄越长，所以"长"后来引申为"长久"之义。

The written form of "长" on oracle bone and bronze is like a person with long hair. People in ancient times never cut hair, so the longer the hair was, the older the people was. On this account, "长" has been extended to mean "lasting ".

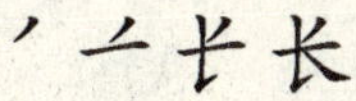

班长	bānzhǎng	monitor
部长	bùzhǎng	minister
队长	duìzhǎng	team leader
成长	chéngzhǎng	grow up
生长	shēngzhǎng	grow
增长	zēngzhǎng	increase
长期	chángqī	long term
长途	chángtú	long distance
延长	yáncháng	prolong

以长为声符的字 Characters with "长" to signify pronunciation	声符在右：张 zhāng
小提示 Tips	"长"的繁体字字形是"長"；"张"与"长"的声母、韵母相同，声调不同。 The original complex form of "长" is "長"; "张" takes "长" as radical. The two characters have same initial and final sounds, while their tones are different.

	廠	厂 chǎng
	楷书（繁体） Regular script（complex form）	楷书（简体） Regular script （simplified form）
	“厂”的繁体字字形是“廠”，由形符“广”和声符“敞”组成，在古代汉语中指简陋的房屋或牲畜圈等。在现代汉语中，其通常指工人从事劳动的场所，如工厂、厂房等。 The original complex form of “厂” is “廠”, made up of “广” and “敞”. In ancient Chinese, it meant simple house or table. In modern Chinese, it indicates some places where workers are working.	一厂

工厂　gōngchǎng　factory	我家附近新建了一家工厂。 Wǒ jiā fùjìn xīnjiàn le yījiā gōngchǎng. A new factory was established near my home.

小提示 Tips	“厂”的繁体字字形是“廠”。 The original complex form of “厂” is “廠”.

<table>
<tr><td rowspan="2"> </td><td> </td><td> </td><td> </td><td>車</td><td>车 chē</td></tr>
<tr><td>甲骨文
Oracle
bone script</td><td>金文
Bronze
inscriptions</td><td>小篆
Small
seal script</td><td>楷书（繁体）
Regular script
(complex form)</td><td>楷书（简体）
Regular script
(simplified form)</td></tr>
<tr><td colspan="5">“车”，甲骨文和金文中，象古代的马车之形，有两轮、车轴及车厢。
The earliest form of “车” is a pictograph of an ancient cart, which represents a bird’s eye view of a cart, showing its body, the two wheels and the axle.</td><td>一 𠂉 𠂉 车</td></tr>
<tr><td colspan="3">车站 chēzhàn station/stop
电车 diànchē trolleybus
火车 huǒchē train
卡车 kǎchē truck
汽车 qìchē automobile
自行车 zìxíngchē bicycle
出租汽车 chūzū qìchē taxi
公共汽车 gōnggòng qìchē bus</td><td colspan="3">车间 chējiān workshop</td></tr>
<tr><td>以车为意符的字
Characters with “车” to signify meaning</td><td colspan="5">意符在左：辅　较　辆　轻　输
意符在右上角：连</td></tr>
<tr><td>小提示
Tips</td><td colspan="5">“车”的繁体字字形是“車”；由“车”组成的字，大多与车或车的动作有关，如：辆、辅、输。
The original complex form of “车” is “車”; the characters with “车” mostly refer to vehicle or transport, such as “辆”, “辅” and “输”.</td></tr>
</table>

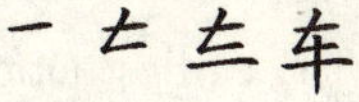

甲骨文 Oracle bone script	金文 Bronze inscriptions	小篆 Small seal script	楷书 Regular script
			出 chū

"出"，甲骨文和金文字形中，上面的部件表示脚，下面的部件表明凹陷处或房子门口，上下两部分合起来表示"脚从凹陷处出来"或"人从房门出来"，后引申为"从里面走出到外面"。

The earliest form of "出" is composed of two parts: the upper part is a pictograph of foot, and the down part represents a hollow. The two parts are put together to mean "get out of hollow", later it extends to express "go or come out of inside".

出发	chūfā	set off/ start out	出版	chūbǎn	to publish
出来	chūlái	come out	出口	chūkǒu	exit / to export
出去	chūqù	go out	出生	chūshēng	to be born
出现	chūxiàn	appear	出院	chūyuàn	to leave hospital
演出	yǎnchū	perform	发出	fāchū	to send out
出租汽车	chūzū qìchē	taxi	突出	tūchū	prominent/give prominence to
			展出	zhǎnchū	to exhibit/to be on show
			指出	zhǐchū	to point out

以出为声符的字 Characters with "出" to signify pronunciation	声符在右：础　chǔ
小提示 Tips	"出"的第三笔一竖要一笔写下来，不能断开。 The third stroke of "出" should be written from top to bottom without being broken.

甲骨文 Oracle bone script	金文 Bronze inscriptions	小篆 Small seal script	楷书 Regular script
			大 dà dài

"大"，甲骨文和金文中，象一个成年人两手两脚张开站立之形。在小篆和楷书字形中，代表上肢的两画被拉直变成一横。古人用"大人"的形象来表示"大"这一抽象意义。

The ancient written form of "大" is in the shape of a man standing with two hands and feet apart. In small seal script and regular script, the two strokes in upper part, symbol of two hands, linked and became one. Ancients used the image of adult to imply big things.

一 ナ 大

			不大	bùdà	not very/not often
大家	dàjiā	everyone	大胆	dàdǎn	fearless
大概	dàgài	probably	大多数	dàduōshù	majority
大声	dàshēng	loud/loudly	大会	dàhuì	general meeting
大学	dàxué	university	大小	dàxiǎo	size
伟大	wěidà	great	大型	dàxíng	large
大夫	dàifu	doctor	扩大	kuòdà	enlarge
			强大	qiángdà	strong

以大为意符的字 Characters with "大" to signify meaning	意符在上：太 意符在下：夫　天 意符在内：因
小提示 Tips	"大"在下面加一点变成"太"（tài），在上面加一横变成"天"（tiān）。 "大" with an added dot under is "太", with an added line over is "天".

			單	单 dān
甲骨文 Oracle bone script	金文 Bronze inscriptions	小篆 Small seal script	楷书（繁体） Regular script (complex form)	楷书（简体） Regular script (simplified form)

“单”，甲骨文和金文中，字形上部像带有两个耳朵的网子，下部是木柄。古人通常用它来捕鸟，所以“单”的本义指捕鸟的工具。因为这种工具往往一次只能捕到一只鸟，由此引申出“单独”、“单一”之义。

The earliest form of “单” is a pictograph of a device for capturing birds, therefore originally “单” means “trammel net”. As this net just could catch one bird at a time, “单” extends to mean “single” or “exclusive”.

简单	jiǎndān	simple	单词	dāncí	word
			单调	dāndiào	monotony
			单位	dānwèi	unit

小提示 Tips	“单”的繁体字字形为“單”。 The original complex form of “单” is “單”.

				刀 dāo
甲骨文 1 Oracle bone script 1	甲骨文 2 Oracle bone script 2	小篆 Small seal script	隶书 Clerical script	楷书 Regular script

“刀”，甲骨文中象刀子之形，上部是刀柄，下部是刀头，也就是带“刀”的部分。到了小篆，刀柄变得弯曲，但还能看出刀的样子。楷书则一点也不象形了。 The earliest form of “刀” is a pictograph of a knife. The upper part is the handle, and the lower portion stands for the edge point. Later its form has a little change that the handle is curved. Then people produce the regular form: “刀”, which isn’t like a knife any more.	𠃌 刀

刀子 dāozi knife	他用一把刀子将苹果切开。 Tā yòng yībǎ dāozi jiāng píngguǒ qiēkāi. He cleaved an apple with a knife.

以刀为意符的字 Characters with “刀” to signify meaning	意符在右：初 切 刮 划 刻 利 意符在下：分 意符在右上角：解 绍

小提示 Tips	“刀”作为偏旁，有时写作“刂”，如上面提到的：刮、划、刻。这是汉字在从隶书到楷书演化的过程中形成的。 As a radical, “刀” is sometimes written as “刂”, such as the characters “刮”, “划” and “刻”; these changes happened during the characters pattern from clerical script to regular script.

	甲骨文 Oracle bone script	金文 Bronze inscriptions	小篆 Small seal script	楷书 Regular script
				弟 dì

"弟"，甲骨文和金文中，字形的中间部分像长木橛，且缠上了绳索。所以，"弟"的本义指"梯子"。因"梯子"是依次而上的，故"弟"引申有"次第"之义。后来用"弟"指"兄弟"或"弟弟"是记音。

The earliest form of "弟" is like a peg bound with ropes. Originally "弟" means ladder. As the rungs of a ladder are upward in proper order, "弟" is extended to mean order. Later it is used to indicate younger brother.

丶 丷 当 当 弓 弟 弟

弟弟 dìdi younger brother

兄弟 xiōngdì brothers

小提示 Tips

"弟"中间的一竖与第三笔横折中的横相接，但不出头。

The vertical stroke in the middle of "弟" connects with the horizontal turning without going across it.

			電	电 diàn
甲骨文 Oracle bone script	金文 Bronze inscriptions	小篆 Small seal script	楷书（繁体） Regular script (complex form)	楷书（简体） Regular script (simplified form)

"电"，甲骨文是闪电之形。金文字形中，上部加上了"雨"，表示下雨才会出现闪电。小篆中，下部表示闪电的部件已发生变化，不似闪电了。

The earliest form of "电" is an ideograph, made up of two parts. The upper portion indicates it is raining, and the lower part is a pictograph of a flash of lightning. The two parts put together to express "lightning".

丨 冂 冃 日 电

电车	diànchē	tramcar/ trolleybus
电灯	diàndēng	electric light
电话	diànhuà	telephone
电视	diànshì	television
电影	diànyǐng	movie
电报	diànbào	telegraph
电台	diàntái	broadcasting station
电梯	diàntī	elevator/lift
电冰箱	diànbīngxiāng	refrigerator
电风扇	diànfēngshàn	electric fan
电视台	diànshìtái	television station
电影院	diànyǐngyuàn	cinema
公用电话	gōngyòng diànhuà	pay phone

小提示 Tips

"电"的繁体字字形是"電"。

The original complex form of "电" is "電".

				東	东 dōng
	甲骨文 Oracle bone script	金文 Bronze inscriptions	小篆 Small seal script	楷书（繁体） Regular script (complex form)	楷书（简体） Regular script (simplified form)

“东”，甲骨文和金文中，像一只两端扎紧的袋子。所以“东”最初指无底的袋子，后用来指表示方向的“东西”之“东”，是记音。 The earliest form of “东” is a pictograph of a bag with two ends fastened. Therefore “东” originally means “the bag without bottom”, later it is used to express direction of the east.	一 ⺧ 车 东 东

东边 dōngbiān the east side 东西 dōngxī/dōngxi east and west/thing	东北 dōngběi northeast 东部 dōngbù east 东方 dōngfāng east/the Orient 东面 dōngmiàn the east side 东南 dōngnán southeast

小提示 Tips	“东”的繁体字字形是“東”。 The original complex form of “东” is “東”.

<table>
<tr><td rowspan="2"></td><td></td><td></td><td></td><td>冬 dōng</td></tr>
<tr><td>甲骨文
Oracle bone script</td><td>金文
Bronze inscriptions</td><td>小篆
Small seal script</td><td>楷书
Regular script</td></tr>
<tr><td colspan="4">“冬”，甲骨文中，字形像一条绳子，两端打上结，表示“终结”。冬天是一年的终结，所以用“冬”来指“冬天”。在金文中，加上了“日”这个部件。在小篆中，把“日”换成表示冰上裂纹的“仌”字。楷书字形为了方便书写，又把下面表示冰上裂纹的“仌”改成了两点。
The written form of “冬” in oracle bone is like a rope with knotted ends, therefore it originally means end. As winter is the end of a year, people use “冬” to indicate winter. In bronze inscriptions, it was added a component “日”. “日” was replaced by “仌” symbol for ice in the small seal script, and then simplified to two dots.</td><td>丿 ク 夂 冬 冬</td></tr>
<tr><td colspan="2">冬天　dōngtiān</td><td>winter</td><td colspan="2">冬天，许多鸟飞往南方。
Dōngtiān, xǔduō niǎo fēiwǎng nánfāng.
In winter, many birds fly to the south.</td></tr>
<tr><td>以冬为意符的字
Characters with “冬” to signify meaning</td><td colspan="4">意符在右：终</td></tr>
<tr><td>小提示
Tips</td><td colspan="4">“终”（zhōng）以“冬”为偏旁，表示“结束”的意思，“终”与“冬”韵母、声调相同。
“终”, with the radical of “冬”, means finish or end. “终” and “冬” have the same final sounds and tones.</td></tr>
</table>

甲骨文 Oracle bone script	金文 Bronze inscriptions	小篆 Small seal script	楷书（繁体） Regular script （complex form）	楷书（简体） Regular script （simplified form）
			兒	儿 ér

"儿"，甲骨文和金文中，像面朝左站立的婴儿，头顶的中间开口，表示婴儿的头颅骨还没有长好。小篆字形上部，仍然像婴儿的头，但下部已经不像婴儿的身体了。楷书字形，为了书写方便，把表示婴儿头的上部省掉了，演变为现在的形体。

The written form of "儿" in oracle bone script and bronze inscriptions is in the shape of an infant standing with face toward left. The upper part symbolizing infant's head is unclosed, which means its incompletely formed fontanel. In order to write easily, the upper part was omitted.

丿 儿

儿子	érzi	son	儿童	értóng	children
女儿	nǚ'ér	daughter			
这儿	zhèr	here			
那儿	nàr	there			

以儿为意符的字 Characters with "儿" to signify meaning	意符在下：先　元
小提示 Tips	"儿"除了指"人"，还经常作名词、动词或代词的后缀，不自成音节，与前面一个音节合在一起构成带卷舌韵母 r 的音节，如"盆儿"、"玩儿"、"这儿"。 Besides meaning human, "儿" often acts as suffixes of nouns, verbs or pronouns. It can't be pronounced independently but connected with preceding syllable to pronounce the phoneme /r/ with a roll.

			而 ér
甲骨文 Oracle bone script	金文 Bronze inscriptions	小篆 Small seal script	楷书 Regular script

"而"，甲骨文中是下垂的四条线，像人下巴上的胡子，上面一横就是下巴。在金文和小篆中，字形趋向工整对称。到了楷书，已经看不出象形。

The written form of "而" in oracle bone is like beard. The four pendulous strings are the symbol for beard and the upper horizontal stroke is the lower jaw. The form trended to symmetrical in the bronze inscriptions and small seal script.

而且	érqiě	as well as/not only… but also…
然而	rán'ér	however/but
从而	cóng'ér	thus/thereby
因而	yīn'ér	therefore

他学习努力而且虚心。
Tā xuéxí nǔlì érqiě xūxīn.
He studies hard and modestly.

演出结束了，然而无人离席。
Yǎnchū jiéshù le，rán'ér wúrén líxí.
The performance is over, but no one leaves.

小提示
Tips

"而"在现代汉语中通常用作连词。
In modern Chinese，"而" is usually used as a conjunction.

				二 èr
	甲骨文 Oracle bone script	金文 Bronze inscriptions	小篆 Small seal script	楷书 Regular script

“二”，甲骨文、金文和小篆的字形都相同，画等长的两横表示数字“二”。楷书字形有细微差别，上面一横比下面一横稍短。“二”最初也是记数符号，后来引申有“不一样”、“不专一”等意义。

The ancient form of “二” is to draw two equilong lines. The regular form changs a little that the upper line is shorter than the lower. Originally “二” is used to indicate two, then it extends to mean “different” or “liable to change”.

一 二

接二连三 jiē' èrliánsān one after the other 一干二净 yīgān' èrjìng thoroughly or completely 二氧化碳 èryǎnghuàtàn carbon dioxide	事故接二连三地发生。 Shìgù jiē' èrliánsān de fāshēng. The accidents came thick and fast.

小提示 Tips	“二”在书写时，先写上横，再写下横。上横短，下横长。 The character begins with the top horizontal stroke, ends up with the longer stroke underneath.

甲骨文	金文	小篆	楷书
			 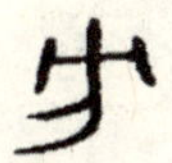   方 fāng
甲骨文 Oracle bone script	金文 Bronze inscriptions	小篆 Small seal script	楷书 Regular script

"方"，甲骨文和金文中，象古代的劳动工具耒耜之形，所以耕田时所起之土称为"方"。后来，"方"用来指"方形"、"方向"等意义是记音。

The earliest form of "方" is a pictograph of an ancient ploughs and plowshares, so originally the soil plowed by ploughs is called "方". And it widens its scope to mean region and direction.

地方	dìfāng	place
方便	fāngbiàn	convenient
方法	fāngfǎ	method
方面	fāngmiàn	aspect
方向	fāngxiàng	direction

北方	běifāng	north
东方	dōngfāng	east
南方	nánfāng	south
西方	xīfāng	west
对方	duìfāng	the other side
双方	shuāngfāng	both sides
方案	fāng'àn	blue print
方式	fāngshì	mode
方针	fāngzhēn	guiding principle
立方	lìfāng	cube
平方	píngfāng	square

以方为声符的字 Characters with "方" to signify meaning	声符在右下角：房 fáng 声符在右：访 fǎng 声符在左：放 fàng
小提示 Tips	"方"字上面有一点，"万"字上面没有点。 "万" with a dot on the top becomes "方"。

	𩙿	飛	飛	飞 fēi
	小篆 Small seal script	隶书 Clerical script	楷书（繁体） Regular script （complex form）	楷书（简体） Regular script （simplified form）

在小篆中，“飞”像鸟展翅飞翔的姿态，上面的部件像鸟颈上的羽毛，中间的“丨”像鸟的身体，两旁的部件像分布在身体左右的羽毛。

The character draws its inspiration from the flight of a bird. The middle “丨” represents a bird's body, which has three feathers; the upper stands for the feathers on neck and others on body.

飞 飞 飞

飞机 fēijī airplane	一只鸟儿飞到了树上。 Yīzhī niǎor fēidào le shùshàng. A bird flew onto a tree.

小提示 Tips	“飞”的繁体字字形是“飛”。 The original complex form of “飞” is “飛”.

				非 fēi
	甲骨文 Oracle bone script	金文 Bronze inscriptions	小篆 Small seal script	楷书 Regular script

"非"，甲骨文和金文中，像两片方向相反且向下生长的羽毛，以表示相反和违背，所以"非"的本义指"违背"。

The earliest form of "非" is a picture of two pieces of feathers, which are opposite and grow downward. As a feather directed downward is unusual and against the law of nature, "非" originally means "be contrary to".

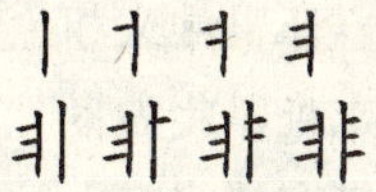

非常 fēicháng very/unusual	非……不可 fēi…bùkě must

以非为声符的字 Characters with "非" to signify pronunciation	声符在右：啡 fēi
小提示 Tips	"非"字左右两边三横之间的距离相等，中间的一横最短，上下两横稍长。 The three horizontal attached to the both verticals of "非" should be arranged with equal space in between. The middle one on both sides is the shortest of all, and the others are a little longer.

	甲骨文 Oracle bone script	金文 Bronze inscriptions	小篆 Small seal script	丰 fēng 楷书 Regular script

"丰"，甲骨文和金文中像一棵树，并且突出了树下部的土堆，所以在甲骨文和金文中，"丰"与"封"意义相同，表示"植树堆土且以此为界"的意思。后"丰"引申指"草木茂盛"，再又引申有"丰满"之义。

The earliest form of "丰" is an ideograph, made up of a tree and a little hillock. Therefore, "丰" meant "planting trees as a boundary between countries" in ancient times. Later "丰" is extended to mean "luxuriant vegetation" or "plentiful".

一 二 三 丰

丰富 fēngfù abundant	这个国家石油资源丰富。 Zhègè guójiā shíyóu zīyuán fēngfù. The country is rich in oil.

小提示 Tips	"丰"的繁体字字形是"豐"。 The original complex form of "丰" is "豐".

<table>
<tr><td rowspan="2"></td><td></td><td></td><td></td><td>夫 fū
fú</td></tr>
<tr><td>甲骨文
Oracle
bone script</td><td>金文
Bronze
inscriptions</td><td>小篆
Small
seal script</td><td>楷书
Regular script</td></tr>
<tr><td colspan="4">“夫”，甲骨文和金文字形像一人正面站立，头上束发戴簪，上面的一横就是发簪。在古代，儿童披发，成年后则要束发戴簪，所以“夫”的本义指“成年男人”。
The earliest form of “夫” is a pictograph of a standing man, whose hair is bound with a hairpin. In ancient times, man should bind their hair when arriving at manhood, therefore “夫” originally means “grown man”.</td><td>一 二 夫 夫</td></tr>
<tr><td colspan="2">大夫　dàfū/dàifu
scholar-bureaucrat/doctor
夫人　fūrén　madam/lady/Mrs.</td><td colspan="3">夫　fú　modal word</td></tr>
<tr><td>小提示
Tips</td><td colspan="4">“夫”常见的有两种读音：第一声“fū”和二声“fú”；“夫”的上横短，下横长，第三笔撇与第一、二横都相交。
“夫” has two pronunciations, while “fū” and “fú” are more commons; The first horizontal stroke of “夫” is shorter than the second one underneath. The left-falling stroke goes across the first two horizontal strokes.</td></tr>
</table>

<table>
<tr><td rowspan="2"></td><td></td><td></td><td></td><td>父 fù</td></tr>
<tr><td>甲骨文
Oracle
bone script</td><td>金文
Bronze
inscriptions</td><td>小篆
Small seal script</td><td>楷书
Regular script</td></tr>
<tr><td colspan="4">“父”，甲骨文和金文中，象手持石斧或棍棒之类器具从事劳作之形。在古代，父亲或男性长辈是野外捕猎劳作的主力，所以用“父”来称呼“父亲”或“男性长辈”。
The earliest form of “父” is a pictograph of a hand holding zax or club or other tools. In ancient times, fathers often hold zax or club to hunt or work. Therefore, “父” is used to call father or male elders.</td><td>丿 八 ⺈ 父</td></tr>
<tr><td colspan="2">父亲　fùqīn　father</td><td colspan="3">伯父　bófù　father's elder brother</td></tr>
<tr><td>以父为意符的字
Characters with “父” to signify meaning</td><td colspan="4">意符在上：爸</td></tr>
<tr><td>小提示
Tips</td><td colspan="4">“父”的第一笔撇与第二笔点相离，第三笔撇与第四笔捺相交。
The first stroke of “父” is a left-falling and the second one is a dot. They are not supposed to be connected. While the lower-left and right-falling strokes go across one another.</td></tr>
</table>

	甲骨文 Oracle bone script	金文 Bronze inscriptions	小篆 Small seal script	干 gān gàn 楷书 Regular script
“干”，甲骨文和金文中，象有枝丫的木棒之形。古人狩猎作战，即以“干”为武器，故本义指“护卫自身的兵器”，后引申有“干预”、“干扰”等意义。 The earliest form of “干” is a pictograph of a limb. In ancient times, people often took limbs as arms to protect themselves, so “干” originally meant “self-protection arms”. By extension, “干” means “intervene or disturb”.				一 二 干
干净 gānjìng clean 干部 gànbù government cadre	饼干 bǐnggān biscuit 干杯 gānbēi cheers 干脆 gāncuì clear-cut/straightforward 干燥 gānzào dry 干吗 gànmá why 能干 nénggàn capable/competent 干活儿 gàn huór do manual work			
小提示 Tips	“干”有两种读音，即“gān”和“gàn”：作形容词时，通常读作“gān”，如“干脆”、“干燥”、“干净”；作动词时，通常读作“gàn”，如“干活”、“干吗”。 “干” have two different readings: “gān” and “gàn”. When used as an adjective to describe dry or lack of water, it should be pronounced as “gān”; when used as a verb to mean work , it should be read “gàn”.			

個	个 gè
楷书（繁体） Regular script （complex form）	楷书（简体） Regular script （simplified form）

“个”的繁体字字形是“個”，声符是“固”。“固”指形状固定之物，“個”指单独个体，所以有“一个”、“一人”之义。现在，“个”通常用作量词。

The original complex form of “个” is “個”, made up of “亻” and “固”. As “固” indicates something having fixed shape and “個” means single unit, so “個” has the meaning of one or one person. Now it is always used as classifier.

丿 人 个

个儿	gèr	stature/size
个性	gèxìng	personality/individuality
个体户	gètǐhù	a small private business
一个劲儿	yígè jìnr	persistently/continues on

小提示 Tips	“个”的繁体字字形是“個”。 The original complex form of “个” is “個”.

	古	工	工	工 gōng
	甲骨文 Oracle bone script	金文 Bronze inscriptions	小篆 Small seal script	楷书 Regular script

"工"，甲骨文字形像斧头一样的工具，金文字形的下部就更像斧头了。小篆字形，为了方便书写，下部的斧头刃变成了一横。"工"本义指"工具"，由此引申指"手持工具干活的人"，如"工匠"、"工人"。

"工" is a pictograph of an ancient work tool, which is like an axe. Later in order to write easily, people modify its lower part to a horizontal and finally "工". Originally it means work tool, then is extended to mean labor, such as workman or worker.

一 丅 工

工厂	gōngchǎng	factory
工人	gōngrén	worker
工业	gōngyè	industry
工作	gōngzuò	work/job
工程	gōngchéng	project
工程师	gōngchéngshī	engineer
工夫	gōngfu	time
工具	gōngjù	tool
工艺品	gōngyìpǐn	art work
工资	gōngzī	salary
加工	jiāgōng	process
人工	réngōng	manpower
施工	shīgōng	construct
手工	shǒugōng	handcraft

小提示 Tips

"工"加上"氵"，是"江"字；加上"纟"，是"红"字；加上"穴"，是"空"字。

"工" becomes "江" by adding "氵", and "红" by adding "纟" on left; when adding "穴" above, it becomes "空".

甲骨文 Oracle bone script	金文 Bronze inscriptions	小篆 Small seal script	公 gōng 楷书 Regular script

"公"，甲骨文的字形像一个大口瓮，上有瓮盖。金文中，下部的瓮口由方形变为圆形。"公"的本义指"瓮"，原始社会用"瓮"储存公共粮食，所以"公"由此引申出"公共"、"公平"之义。
The earliest form of "公" is a pictograph of a big pottery with a cover. Later its lower part is modified to "厶". Originally "公" means pottery. As in ancient times, people usually use it to store public grains, it extends to indicate public or impartial.

丿 八 公 公

公斤	gōngjīn	kilogram
公里	gōnglǐ	kilometer
公园	gōngyuán	park
公尺	gōngchǐ	meter
办公室	bàngōngshì	office
公共汽车	gōnggòng qìchē	bus
办公	bàngōng	work
公费	gōngfèi	at public expense
公共	gōnggòng	public
公开	gōngkāi	to the view
公路	gōnglù	highway
公司	gōngsī	company
公元	gōngyuán	Anno Domini
公用电话	gōngyòng diànhuà	pay phone

小提示 Tips	"公"的上面是"八"，不是"人"或"入"。 The top part of "公" is not "人" or "入" but "八".

金文 1 Bronze inscriptions 1	金文 2 Bronze inscriptions 2	小篆 Small seal script	楷书 Regular script
			共 gòng

"共"在金文和小篆字形中，像双手捧着器物，表示恭敬之义。在楷书中，表示双手的部件笔画拉直省并，成为现在使用的字形"共"。"共"现在通常用来表示"共同"之义。另外又造"恭"字，记录本义"恭敬"。

The ancient written form of "共" is in the shape of two hands holding something to symbol for religiousness respectfully. The strokes of signifying hands are stretched to "共" in regular script form. And now it often means together. People make another character "恭" to mean respectful.

一 十 卄 龷 共 共

一共	yīgòng	altogether
公共汽车	gōnggòng qìchē	bus
公共	gōnggòng	public
共同	gòngtóng	common/jointly
共产党	gòngchǎndǎng	Communist Party

小提示 Tips

"恭"（gōng）、"供"（gōng/gòng）以"共"为偏旁，声母、韵母与"共"相同，声调有差别。

"恭" and "供" take "共" as their radical, and the initial and final sounds are same, while the tones are different.

				廣	广 guǎng
	甲骨文 Oracle bone script	金文 Bronze inscriptions	小篆 Small seal script	楷书（繁体） Regular script (complex form)	楷书（简体） Regular script (simplified form)

"广"，甲骨文字形由表示屋子的形符"宀"和声符"黄"组成。金文和小篆字形中，形符"宀"变为"广"，意义也引申为"广大"、"宽阔"。到了现代汉语中，由于汉字简化，就用了"廣"的形符"广"作为它的简化字形。

In the oracle bone script，"广" is pictogram，made up of "宀" and "黄". Later the pictogram "宀" becomes "广"，and it extends to mean extensive and wide. In modern Chinese，because of simplification of Chinese characters，its pictogram "广" is adopted to be its simplified form.

丶 亠 广

广播 guǎngbō broadcast

广场	guǎngchǎng	a public square
广大	guǎngdà	vast
广泛	guǎngfàn	wide range
广阔	guǎngkuò	wide
广告	guǎnggào	advertisement
推广	tuīguǎng	popularize

小提示 Tips	"广"的繁体字字形是"廣"。 The original complex form of "广" is "廣".

甲骨文 Oracle bone script	金文 Bronze inscriptions	小篆 Small seal script	果 guǒ 楷书 Regular script

"果"，甲骨文象果树上结了很多果实之形。金文省略为一个果实，突出了果实里的果瓣、籽。小篆又省略了果实里的籽。再变为楷书"果"。

The oracle bone script character "果" looks like a tree with lots of fruit. There is only one fruit in bronze inscriptions, but the carpel and seeds are stressed out. And the seed is left out in small seal script , then regular script character "果" comes into being.

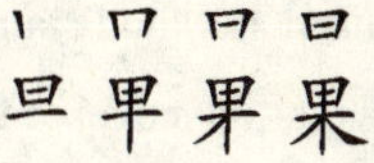

果	guǒ	fruit	果然	guǒrán	as expected
结果	jiéguǒ	result	成果	chéngguǒ	achievement
苹果	píngguǒ	apple	如果	rúguǒ	if
水果	shuǐguǒ	fruit	效果	xiàoguǒ	effect

小提示 Tips	"果"字下端不带钩。 The vertical stroke of "果" is written without a hook.

甲骨文 Oracle bone script	金文 Bronze inscriptions	小篆 Small seal script	楷书 Regular script
			合 hé

“合”，甲骨文、金文和小篆字形接近，上面的部件像器物的盖子，下面的部件像装东西的器物，上下部件合在一起表示“会合”之义。

“合” is a pictograph of an ancient food container. The lower part is used for food, and the upper portion, made up of three lines, represents its cover. The two components joined together means “meet or join”.

合适	héshì	suitable/appropriate
集合	jíhé	congregation/gather

符合	fúhé	come up to/to correspond with
合理	hélǐ	rational/reasonable
合同	hétóng	agreement/contract
合作	hézuò	cooperate/cooperation
结合	jiéhé	unite/be united in wedlock
联合	liánhé	union/combine
配合	pèihé	act in concert with
适合	shìhé	fit/suit/be suitable
综合	zōnghé	to integrate/composite

小提示 Tips

由盖子与器物相合，“合”引申有“配合”之义，再又引申有“合适”之义。

From the image of a right cover for a container, “合” extends to mean matching, and then refers to “suited”.

金文 1	金文 2	小篆	隶书	楷书
			黑	黑 hēi
金文 1 Bronze inscriptions 1	金文 2 Bronze inscriptions 2	小篆 Small seal script	隶书 Clerical script	楷书 Regular script

“黑”，在金文中，上部像烟囱中的点点烟灰，下部是“炎（两个火）”。这就是说，在烧火时，把烟囱里面都熏黑了。在楷书字形中，“炎”下面的“火”写为“灬”，上面的“火”写成了“土”。

The earliest form of “黑” is made up of two parts. The upper part is a pictograph of chimney and the dots inside represents soot. The lower part “炎” indicates fires. The two parts getting together means the chimney is blackened by smoke. Later people modify its lower part: the upper “火” is changed to “土” and the lower “火” becomes “灬”, to the regular form “黑”.

黑板 hēibǎn blackboard	黑暗 hēi'àn dark

小提示 Tips	“黑”的上部不是“里”。 It should be noted that the upper part of “黑” is not “里”.

小篆 1 Small seal script 1	小篆 2 Small seal script 2	楷书 Regular script
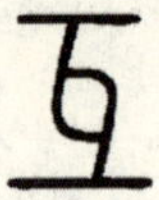	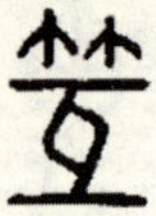	互 hù

"互"，古代字形像卷绳子的工具。中间部分就是把手，将绳线缠在上下的部分，因此"互"有"交互"、"相互"等意义。

The ancient form of "互" is a pictograph of a tool that is used to wind ropes. The middle part of "互" is the handle, and the upper and lower part are where the ropes wind around. Therefore, "互" means "mutual" or "each other".

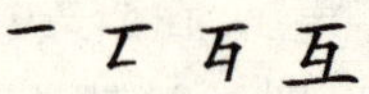

互相 hùxiāng each other	相互 xiānghù each other

小提示 Tips

"互"的第二笔是撇折，第三笔是横折，横折的竖笔稍向左下倾斜。

The second stroke of "互" is a left-falling turning, and the vertical part of the horizontal turning slants to the lower left.

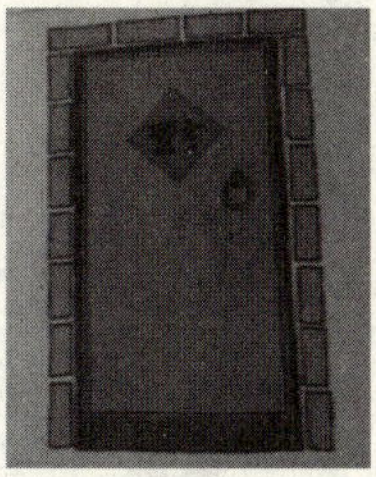	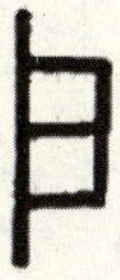	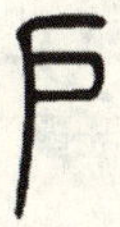	户 hù
	甲骨文 Oracle bone script	小篆 Small seal script	楷书 Regular script

"户"，甲骨文字形像单扇门。故"户"的本义指"单扇门"，后引申为出入口的通称，如"门户"、"窗户"等，后来又引申指"人家"、"住户"。 The earliest form of "户" is a pictograph of a single leaf door, therefore "户" originally means single door. By extension, it indicates access such as door or window. Then it extends to mean "household".	丶 ㇇ 彐 户

窗户 chuānghù window	打开窗户，让新鲜的空气进来。 Dǎkāi chuānghù, ràng xīnxiān de kōngqì jìnlái. Open the window and let in some fresh air.

以户为意符的字 Characters with "户" to signify meaning	意符在左上角：房
小提示 Tips	"户"在古代指"门"，故经常与"门"连用，如成语"门当户对"、"门户之见"等；凡由"户"字所组成的字大都与"门"、"窗"有关，如"启"、"扉"、"扇"等。 In ancient times, "户" indicated a door, therefore it was usually used with "门", such as "门当户对" and "门户之见"; the characters with "户" mostly refer to a door, such as "启", "扉" and "扇".

甲骨文 Oracle bone script	金文 Bronze inscriptions	小篆 Small seal script	隶书 Clerical script	楷书 Regular script
				黄 huáng

"黄"，在甲骨文和金文中，像腰间挂有佩饰站立着的人，并且突出了腰间的佩饰，故"黄"的本义表示人挂带的佩玉，后用来指黄色，是记音。

The written form of "黄" in oracle bone script and bronze inscriptions is in the shape of a man standing with jade round waist, and the jade is highlighted. "黄" originally means jade, then it is borrowed to mean yellow.

黄瓜	huángguā	cucumber
黄油	huángyóu	butter

吃点黄瓜吧。
Chīdiǎn huángguā ba.
Have some cucumber.

他在面包上涂黄油。
Tā zài miànbāo shàng tú huángyóu.
He spread butter on his bread.

小提示 Tips

"黄"的笔画比较复杂，先上后下。上横短，下横长，中间的"由"写得扁一些。

The strokes of "黄" are rather complex. It can be only written from top to bottom, and the first horizontal stroke is shorter than the lower. The component "由" in the middle should be oblate.

	甲骨文 Oracle bone script	金文 Bronze inscriptions	小篆 Small seal script	楷书 Regular script
				回 huí

"回"，金文中象水面的旋涡，也就是流水的旋转之形。到了小篆，为了看起来规整和书写方便，字形变成了大口套住小口。"回"的本义指"旋转"，现在多用来表示"回来"或"回去"。

The earliest form of "回" is a pictograph of a whirlpool on water. Later in order to write easily and look standard, people change its form to two "口": the smaller one in the bigger one. Originally "回" means "whirl", and now it is often used to express "come back" or "go back".

回答	huídá	answer	回头	huítóu	turn one's head
回来	huílái	come back	回信	huíxìn	write back
回去	huíqù	go back	回忆	huíyì	recall

小提示 Tips

"回"字先写外面的大"口"，但不封口，再写里面的小"口"，最后外面的大"口"才封口。

The outside big "口" is written first but without the final stroke, then write the inside small "口" and finally finish the outside "口".

	甲骨文 Oracle bone script	金文 Bronze inscriptions	小篆 Small seal script	楷书（繁体） Regular script (complex form)	楷书（简体） Regular script (simplified form)
				會	会 huì

"会"，甲骨文和金文字形分三部分，上部像盖子，下部是底儿，中间像装着一些东西。小篆字形中，下部变成了"日"字。"会"的本义指"上下相合"，所以引申有"会合"、"聚合"之义。

The earliest form of "会" is a pictograph of a box with something inside. The upper part is the cover, the lower part is the bottom, and the middle part is something in it. Later the lower part is modified to "日". Originally "会" means cover lid, then is extended to mean "meet" or "get together".

丿 人 亼 亼 会 会

会话	huìhuà	conversation
机会	jīhuì	chance
社会	shèhuì	society
晚会	wǎnhuì	party
宴会	yànhuì	banquet
一会儿	yīhuìr	for a moment
大会	dàhuì	general meeting
会客	huìkè	receive a visitor
会谈	huìtán	talks
会议	huìyì	meeting
开会	kāihuì	have a meeting
体会	tǐhuì	experience
误会	wùhuì	misunderstand/misunderstanding
约会	yuēhuì	date/dating
运动会	yùndònghuì	sports meeting
展览会	zhǎnlǎnhuì	exhibition

小提示 Tips	"会"的繁体字字形是"會"。The original complex form of "会" is "會".

				火 huǒ
	甲骨文1 Oracle bone script 1	甲骨文2 Oracle bone script 2	小篆 Small seal script	楷书 Regular script

"火"，甲骨文中像架柴生火时的一团火焰，所以本义指物体燃烧时的光和焰。 "火" is a pictograph of fire, produced by lighting a pile of firewood. So originally "火" means the flames or light of burning wood, and now its original meaning is still in use.	丶 丷 火 火
火车 huǒchē train	火柴 huǒchái match
以火为意符的字 Characters with "火" to signify meaning	意符在左边：灯 烦 炼 烧 意符在下边：黑 然 热 熟 照
小提示 Tips	为了书写的方便，"火"作为偏旁在隶书中有时写作"灬"并沿用至今，如："黑"、"然"、"热"。 For convenience, "火" as a radical sometimes is written as "灬" in clerical script which has been retained today, such as "黑", "然" and "热".

<table>
<tr><td rowspan="3"></td><td></td><td>几 jī
jǐ</td></tr>
<tr><td>小篆
Small seal script</td><td>楷书
Regular script</td></tr>
<tr><td>“几”，小篆字形像可以摆放物件的小桌子，所以本义指一种器具，如“桌几”、“茶几”等。
The small seal form of “几” is a pictograph of a table, therefore “几” indicates a piece of furniture, such as “small table” or “tea table”.</td><td>丿 几</td></tr>
</table>

<table>
<tr><td>几乎 jīhū nearly/almost</td><td>海洋几乎占了地球表面的四分之三。
Hǎiyáng jīhū zhàn le dìqiú biǎomiàn de sì fēn zhī sān.
The sea covers nearly three-fourths of the world's surface.</td></tr>
<tr><td>以几为声符的字
Characters with “几” to signify pronunciation</td><td>声符在右：机 jī</td></tr>
<tr><td>小提示
Tips</td><td>“几”是多音字：指器具如“茶几”、“炕几”等时，读为“jī”；作疑问词用来询问数目如“几个”、“几天”等时，读为“jǐ”。
“几” has two different readings. When indicating tea table, it reads “jī”; when it is used as a interrogative, it should be pronounced as “jǐ”.</td></tr>
</table>

<table>
<tr><td rowspan="2"></td><td>己</td><td>己</td><td>己</td><td>己 jǐ</td></tr>
<tr><td>甲骨文
Oracle
bone script</td><td>金文
Bronze
inscriptions</td><td>小篆
Small
seal script</td><td>楷书
Regular script</td></tr>
<tr><td colspan="4">“己”，甲骨文、金文、小篆和楷书的字形均相近，象系在箭上的弯弯曲曲的丝绳之形，故本义指“拴在箭上的丝绳”，后来指“自己”的“己”是记音。
The ancient form of “己” is a pictograph of curving ropes tying to an arrow, so it originally means the ropes tying to arrow. Later it is used to indicate oneself.</td><td>ㄱ ㄱ 己</td></tr>
<tr><td colspan="2">自己　zìjǐ　oneself</td><td colspan="3">他建立了自己的公司。
Tā jiànlì le zìjǐ de gōngsī.
He has established his own firm.</td></tr>
<tr><td>以己为声符的字
Characters with “己” to signify pronunciation</td><td colspan="4">声符在右：记　jì　纪　jì</td></tr>
<tr><td>小提示
Tips</td><td colspan="4">“己”、“已”、“巳”三者字形相似，要注意区别：“己”最后一笔不出头，“已”出一点，“巳”则完全相连。
“己”，“已” and “巳” are so similar as to be easily confused. It should be noted that the last stroke of “己” is not over the second stroke, and the last stroke of “已” is a little over, while “巳” is totally linked with the first stroke.</td></tr>
</table>

	甲骨文 Oracle bone script	金文 Bronze inscriptions	小篆 Small seal script	楷书（繁体）Regular script (complex form)	楷书（简体）Regular script (simplified form)
				見	见 jiàn

“见”，甲骨文和金文中，像一人侧身而坐，突出头部的眼睛，以表明用眼睛看的意义，所以“见”的本义是“看”、“看见”。

The earliest form of “见” is a pictograph of a man sitting sideways with his eye highlighted. Therefore, “见” originally means “to look or to see”.

丨 冂 贝 见

见面	jiànmiàn	meet/see somebody
看见	kànjiàn	to see/to catch sight of
听见	tīngjiàn	hear
意见	yìjiàn	opinion
再见	zàijiàn	good bye
会见	huìjiàn	interview
接见	jiējiàn	grant an interview to
遇见	yùjiàn	meet/come across
碰见	pèngjiàn	meet unexpectedly

以见为意符的字
Characters with “见” to signify meaning

意符在右：观　视
意符在下：觉　览

小提示
Tips

“见”的繁体字字形是“見”；由“见”组成的字，其字义大多与“用眼睛看”有关。

The traditional form of “见” is “見”; characters with “见” usually refer to looking.

	[illegible]	[illegible]	[illegible]	交	交 jiāo
	甲骨文 Oracle bone script	金文 Bronze inscriptions	小篆 Small seal script	隶书 Clerical script	楷书 Regular script

"交"，甲骨文、金文和小篆字形，像一个人正面双腿交叉站立。所以，"交"本义指"交叉"或"交错"。如果交叉则双腿必然相接触，"交"由此又引申指人与人之间的接触活动，如"交往"、"交流"、"交际"等。 The earliest written form of "交" is like a man standing with his legs crossed, therefore "交" originally means cross. When cross, people's legs are certain contacted, which extends to indicate the contact between people, such as "交往" (associate), "交流" (exchange) and "交际" (communication).	丶 亠 六 六 亣 交

交流　jiāoliú　exchange 交换　jiāohuàn　to exchange 交际　jiāojì　social intercourse 交通　jiāotōng　traffic 外交　wàijiāo　diplomacy	文化交流是国与国之间建立联系的桥梁。 Wénhuà jiāoliú shì guó yǔ guó zhījiān jiànlì liánxì de qiáoliáng. Cultural exchange is a way of building bridges between nations.

以交为声符的字 Characters with "交" to signify pronunciation	声符在右：饺　jiǎo　较　jiào
小提示 Tips	交的第三笔撇和第四笔点相离，第五笔撇和第六笔捺相交。 Under the horizontal stroke of "交", the left-falling and the dot on the right are not connected, but the lower left-falling stroke goes across the right-falling one.

				角 jiǎo
	甲骨文 Oracle bone script	金文 Bronze inscriptions	小篆 Small seal script	楷书 Regular script

"角"，甲骨文和金文字形都像一只兽角，中间的曲线像角上的纹理，所以"角"的本义指动物头上的角。
"角" is a pictograph of an animal horn, such as a bull's or a goat's, and the curves in the middle stand for their horns' grain. Therefore, "角" originally means animal's horns.

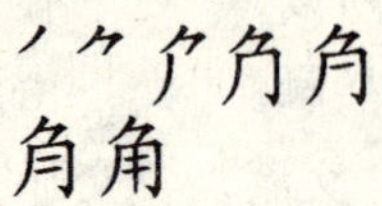

角度 jiǎodù angel/point of view 角落 jiǎoluò corner	三角 sānjiǎo a triangle
以角为意符的字 Characters with "角" to signify meaning	意符在左：解
小提示 Tips	"角"的第一笔与第二笔相接，下部是"用"。 The first two strokes of "角" are connected , and the lower part is "用".

					介 jiè
	甲骨文 1 Oracle bone script 1	甲骨文 2 Oracle bone script 2	小篆 Small seal script	隶书 Clerical script	楷书 Regular script
"介"，甲骨文和金文中，像一人侧面而立，身体前后穿着铠甲，因古代武士的铠甲通常由一片片皮革缀成，字形上用"∷"表示。"介"的本义指"铠甲"。 The earliest form of "介" is a pictograph of a standing man, who faced left and girded himself with armor. In ancient times, armor was made of flakes of leathers, which were represented by "∷". It originally means "armor".					丿 人 介 介

介绍 jièshào to introduce/introduction	他向我们简要地介绍了一下他的公司。 Tā xiàng wǒmen jiǎnyào de jièshào le yīxià tā de gōngsī. He gave us a brief introduction about his company.
以介为声符的字 Characters with "介" to signify pronunciation	声符在下：界 jiè
小提示 Tips	在现代汉语中，"介"通常指"介绍"、"媒介"之义。 In modern Chinese, "介" usually means "to introduce" or "medium".

	𠂆	斤	斤	斤	斤 jīn
	甲骨文 Oracle bone script	金文 Bronze inscriptions	小篆 Small seal script	隶书 Clerical script	楷书 Regular script

"斤"，甲骨文象斧具之形，箭头表示斧刃，斧柄弯曲。金文将斧刃与斧柄分开了。小篆更不象形，由小篆演变为隶书、楷书字形。用来指重量单位"公斤"中的"斤"是记音。

The oracle bone script character "斤" looks like an axe, the arrow standing for axe blade, helve curved. The axe blade and helve are separated in bronze inscriptions. Pictograph is no longer in use in small seal script and clerical script. And it is used as the unit of weight afterwards.

㇒ 厂 斤 斤

斤 jīn a unit of weight（=1/2 kilogram） 公斤 gōngjīn kilogram	这些苹果每公斤五元。 zhèixiē píngguǒ měi gōngjīn wǔyuán. These apples cost five yuan per kilogram.
以斤为意符的字 Characters with "斤" to signify meaning	意符在右：所 新
以斤为声符的字 Characters with "斤" to signify pronunciation	声符在右上角：近 jìn

甲骨文 Oracle bone script	金文 Bronze inscriptions	小篆 Small seal script	隶书 Clerical script	今 jīn 楷书 Regular script

“今”，甲骨文和金文中，字形像有舌有钮的铃铛。后来指“现在”、“现代”等意义，是记音。

The earliest form of “今” is a pictograph of a tinkle bell. Later “今” is used to express “now” or “modern”.

丿 人 亽 今

今年	jīnnián	this year
今天	jīntiān	today
今后	jīnhòu	from now on
如今	rújīn	nowadays
至今	zhìjīn	up to now

小提示
Tips

要注意“今”与“令”的区别。
It should be noted that “今” and “令” are different.

甲骨文 Oracle bone script	金文 Bronze inscriptions	小篆 Small seal script	九 jiǔ 楷书 Regular script

“九”，甲骨文和金文字形基本相同，像弯曲的手肘，故“九”本义指“手肘”，后来指数字“九”是记音。 The earliest form of “九” is a pictograph of a human’s elbow. So it originally means elbow, and later is used to indicate nine.	丿 九
九月 jiǔyuè September	炎热的天气持续到了九月。 Yánrè de tiānqì chíxù dàole jiǔyuè. The hot weather lasted until September.
以九为声符的字 Characters with “九” to signify pronunciation	声符在下：究 jiū
小提示 Tips	“九”在书写时，第一笔撇与第二笔横折弯钩的横笔部分相交。 The left vertical falling of “九” goes across the horizontal part of its second stroke.

久 jiǔ

小篆 Small seal script	楷书 Regular script

“久”，小篆字形中，上部像卧着的人，末端一笔像用物灼烧身体。因为古人治病，常燃艾灼烧身体，故“久”的本义指“灸灼”，后用来指“长久”之义，是记音。

The ancient form of “久” is composed of two parts: the upper part is like a man lying, and the down stroke is like burning the man’s hip with something. As ancients often use burning wormwood to treat illness by fumigating their bodies, “久” originally means “cauterize”, later is used to express “permanent”.

ノ ク 久

不久 bùjiǔ soon/ not long (after)

好久 hǎojiǔ quite a while

悠久 yōujiǔ long-standing/age-old

小提示
Tips

在现代汉语中，“久”通常指“时间长”，例如：“不久”、“好久”、“悠久”等。

In modern Chinese, “久” usually means long time, such as “不久”, “好久” and “悠久”.

			開	开 kāi
	小篆 1 Small seal script 1	小篆 2 Small seal script 2	楷书（繁体） Regular script （complex form）	楷书（简体） Regular script （simplified form）

“开”，从小篆字形 2 中，可以看出象用双手推开门之形，所以“开”的本义是“开门”，也正是由“开门”这个动作创造出“开”的字形。后来“开”又引申有“张开”、“分开”等意义。
The ancient form of “开” is composed of two components：the inside part is a pictograph of a pair of hands，and the outside part represents double swing doors. The two parts are put together to mean “open（the）door”. Later it is extended to express “spread” or “separate ”.

一 二 于 开

开始	kāishǐ	begin/beginning
开学	kāixué	school opens/term begins
离开	líkāi	leave
开玩笑	kāi wánxiào	to play a joke

公开	gōngkāi	public/make public
开放	kāifàng	be open to the public
开会	kāihuì	have a meeting
开课	kāikè	give a course
开明	kāimíng	open-minded
开辟	kāipì	open up
开演	kāiyǎn	to begin
开展	kāizhǎn	to launch
展开	zhǎnkāi	to unfold/to carry out
召开	zhàokāi	to convoke

小提示 Tips	“开”的繁体字字形是“開”。 The original complex form of “开” is “開”.

甲骨文 Oracle bone script	小篆 Small seal script	隶书 Clerical script	楷书 Regular script
			口 kǒu

"口"，甲骨文和小篆都象嘴巴之形，嘴角上翘。隶书用直笔方折取代了小篆的弧笔圆折，变为今文。

"口" in oracle bone script and small seal script both like mouth with corners turned up. In clerical script, strokes of "口" become straight. Then it is evolved into the modern character.

口	kǒu	mouth
口语	kǒuyǔ	spoken language
门口	ménkǒu	doorway
口袋	kǒudài	pocket
口号	kǒuhào	slogan
进口	jìnkǒu	entrance
出口	chūkǒu	exit
人口	rénkǒu	population

以口为意符的字 Characters with "口" to signify meaning	意符在上中下：号 虽 只 哭 器 问 告 各 名 意符在左：啊 吧 唱 吃 吹 哈 喊 喝 叫 咳 啦 吗 哪 呐 呢 嗯 啤 听 喂 响 呀 咱 咖啡 意符在右：和 加 如 知
以口为声符的字 Characters with "口" to signify pronunciation	声符在右：扣 kòu

甲骨文 Oracle bone script	金文 Bronze inscriptions	小篆 Small seal script	楷书 Regular script
			来 lái

"来"，甲骨文和金文中，象笔直向上的小麦之形。"来"的本义指"小麦"，后指"来往"是记音。现在通常用作动词，表"由彼至此"、"由远及近"。

The earliest form of "来" is a pictograph of wheat, so originally "来" indicates wheat. Later it is used to express "come or arrive", and its original meaning gradually is out of people's mind. Now it is used as a verb to indicate "come".

出来	chūlái	come out
过来	guòlái	come over
回来	huílái	come back
将来	jiānglái	in the future
进来	jìnlái	come in
起来	qǐlái	stand up
上来	shànglái	come up
下来	xiàlái	come down
原来	yuánlái	turn out to be/used to be

本来	běnlái	from the beginning/ originally
从来	cónglái	always/at all times
后来	hòulái	afterwards/later/then
未来	wèilái	future/coming
近来	jìnlái	recently
看来	kànlái	seemingly/it looks as if
来信	láixìn	incoming letter
来自	láizì	come from
以来	yǐlái	since
来得及	láidejí	in time
来不及	láibùjí	be late for
越来越	yuèláiyuè	more and more

小提示 Tips	"来"的繁体字字形是"來"。 The original complex form of "来" is "來".

<table>
<tr><td rowspan="2"></td><td></td><td></td><td></td><td></td><td>老 lǎo</td></tr>
<tr><td>甲骨文
Oracle bone script</td><td>金文
Bronze inscriptions</td><td>小篆
Small seal script</td><td>隶书
Clerical script</td><td>楷书
Regular script</td></tr>
<tr><td colspan="5">“老”，在甲骨文中，象头发很长、拄着拐杖的老人之形。上面的部件像老人的长发，下面的部件像老人拄着拐杖伛偻的身躯，所以“老”就是指“老人”。
The ancient written form of “老” is in the shape of an old man with long hair. The upper part is like the man’s hair and the lower part is like his hunchbacked body with crutch, so “老” means old people.</td><td>一 十 土 耂 老</td></tr>
<tr><td colspan="2">老师　lǎoshī　teacher</td><td colspan="4">古老　gǔlǎo　ancient/age-old
老是　lǎoshì　always
老百姓　lǎobǎixìng　citizen
老板　lǎobǎn　boss
老虎　lǎohǔ　tiger
老人　lǎorén　old people/the aged
老实　lǎoshi　veracity</td></tr>
<tr><td>小提示
Tips</td><td colspan="5">“老”的第四笔撇与第三横相交。第五笔短撇与末笔竖弯钩相接。下面是“匕”，不是“七”。
The left-falling stroke of “老” goes across the horizontal. Its left-falling short stroke is connected with the final vertical upward turning. The lower part is not “七” but “匕”.</td></tr>
</table>

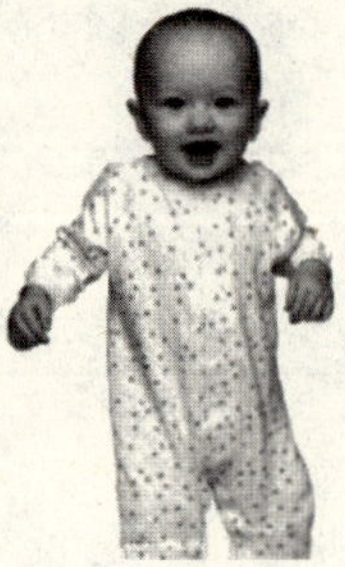

小篆 Small seal script	隶书 Clerical script	了 liǎo le 楷书 Regular script

"了"，小篆字形像是没有手臂的小孩子，表示刚出生的幼婴。婴儿出生后性别就能看清楚，所以引申为"了解"、"了然"之义。现在表示动作的完成，或用作表示完成时态的助词。

The ancient form of "了" is like an infant without arms. When the baby was born, the sex was clear, so "了" was extended to mean "understand" or "be clear". And now it is used to express "to finish or make a decision", or as a particle to be used in perfect tense.

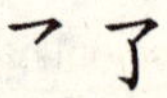

乛 了

了解	liǎojiě	understand
为了	wèile	in order to
……极了……	…jíle…	extremely
除了……以外	chúle…yǐwài	besides
算了	suànle	let it pass
不得了	bùdéliǎo	desperately serious
了不起	liǎobùqǐ	extraordinary

小提示 Tips

"了"有两种读音："liǎo"和"le"。当它处于词头时，通常读"liǎo"，如："了解"、"了不起"；当它处于词尾时，通常读"le"，如："为了"、"除了"、"算了"。

"了" has two different readings: "liǎo" and "le". When as an initial word, it should be read "liǎo", and at the end of a word, it is usually pronounced as "le".

<table>
<tr><td rowspan="2"> </td><td> </td><td> </td><td> </td><td> </td><td>力 lì</td></tr>
<tr><td>甲骨文
Oracle
bone script</td><td>金文
Bronze
inscriptions</td><td>小篆
Small
seal script</td><td>隶书
Clerical
script</td><td>楷书
Regular script</td></tr>
<tr><td colspan="5">“力”，甲骨文和金文的形体像耕田用的犁，上部长长的弯曲部分是犁把，下部是犁田的犁头。所以“力”的本义是指犁田的工具，因犁田要用力，由此引申出“力量”之义。
The earliest form of “力” is a pictograph of a plough. The upper part represents the plough handle, and the lower part indicates the plowshare. Therefore, “力” originally means plough. To plough field needs power, so “力” is extended to mean power.</td><td>フ力</td></tr>
<tr><td colspan="3">努力 nǔlì make great efforts</td><td colspan="3">风力 fēnglì wind force
精力 jīnglì energy
力量 lìliàng force
力气 lìqi physical strength
能力 nénglì capability
用力 yònglì exert oneself (physically)
有力 yǒulì forceful
力所能及 lìsuǒnéngjí
as one's capacity allows</td></tr>
<tr><td colspan="2">以力为意符的字
Characters with “力”
to signify meaning</td><td colspan="4">意符在左：加
意符在右：动 助
意符在下：男 劳 努 务</td></tr>
<tr><td colspan="2">小提示
Tips</td><td colspan="4">由“力”组成的字，大都与“力量”和“行动”有关，如上面提到的那些字。
Characters with “力”, such as those mentioned above, mostly refer to “strength” or “action”.</td></tr>
</table>

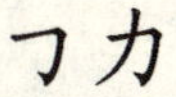

<table>
<tr><td rowspan="2"></td><td></td><td></td><td></td><td>立 lì</td></tr>
<tr><td>甲骨文
Oracle
bone script</td><td>金文
Bronze
inscriptions</td><td>小篆
Small
seal script</td><td>楷书
Regular script</td></tr>
<tr><td colspan="4">“立”，甲骨文和金文中，上部是正面站立的人形，下面一横指地面，所以“立”本义指人站立于地面。小篆中，身体与双腿省并，人的形体发生了一些变化。到了楷书，笔画拉直，变为现在的字形“立”。
The ancient written form of “立” is in the shape of a man standing on the ground, so it originally means people on the ground. The strokes of “立” symbolize people's body and both legs mix in small seal script, later become straight in regular script.</td><td>丶 亠 亣 方 立</td></tr>
<tr><td colspan="2">立刻 lìkè immediately/at once</td><td colspan="3">成立 chénglì establish/set up
独立 dúlì independent/independently
建立 jiànlì build
立场 lìchǎng position/standpoint
立方 lìfāng cube
立即 lìjí immediately</td></tr>
<tr><td>以立为意符的字
Characters with “立” to signify meaning</td><td colspan="4">意符在右：位
意符在左：站</td></tr>
<tr><td>小提示
Tips</td><td colspan="4">立的第四笔是撇，下横比上横稍长。
The fourth stroke of “立” is left-falling, and the lower horizontal stroke is longer than the upper one.</td></tr>
</table>

<table>
<tr><td rowspan="2"></td><td></td><td></td><td></td><td>两 liǎng</td></tr>
<tr><td>金文 1
Bronze
inscriptions 1</td><td>金文 2
Bronze
inscriptions 2</td><td>小篆
Small
seal script</td><td>楷书
Regular script</td></tr>
<tr><td colspan="4">“两”，金文中象秤砣之形。古代的秤砣由两个小钱合成，小钱的形状像两个“入”字，所以“两”指“斤两”。又因为是由两个小钱合成，所以“两”引申为数目，指“二”。
The earliest form of “两” is a pictograph of an ancient balance weight, which are combined by two copper coins, so “两” originally means weight. As it is made up of two coins, by extension, it indicates “two”.</td><td>一 丅 丙 丙
丙 两 两</td></tr>
<tr><td colspan="2">两旁 liǎngpáng
both sides/either side
有两下子 yǒu liǎngxiàzi
have real skill</td><td colspan="3">两极 liǎngjí the earth's poles/electric poles
两手 liǎngshǒu double tactics
两口子 liǎngkǒuzi husband and wife</td></tr>
<tr><td>以两为意符的字
Characters with “两” to signify meaning</td><td colspan="4">意符在右：俩　辆</td></tr>
<tr><td>小提示
Tips</td><td colspan="4">“两”的繁体字字形是“两”。
The original complex form of “两” is “两”.</td></tr>
</table>

甲骨文 Oracle bone script	金文 Bronze inscriptions	小篆 Small seal script	隶书 Clerical script	楷书 Regular script
				六 liù lù

“六”，甲骨文和金文中，象从侧面看到的房屋之形，本义指“房屋”，后来表示数字“六”，是记音。

The earliest form of “六” is a pictograph of an ancient house viewed from the side. It originally means house, then is used to indicate six.

六月 liùyuè June	他是去年六月开始在这里工作的。 Tā shì qùnián liùyuè kāishǐ zài zhèlǐ gōngzuò de. He started work here last June.

小提示 Tips	“六”有两个读音“liù”和“lù”。一般情况下，都读作“liù”；当用于山名和县名时，才读作“lù”，如“六安”、“六合”。 “六” has two readings, and it usually reads “liù”. When used as a name of a place, it should be pronounced as “lù”, for example, “六安” and “六合”.

				馬	马 mǎ
	甲骨文 Oracle bone script	金文 Bronze script	小篆 Small seal script	楷书（繁体） Regular script （complex form）	楷书（简体） Regular script （simplified form）

"马"，甲骨文、金文是马侧身竖立的样子，突出眼睛与鬃毛。小篆将眼睛与鬃毛连笔了。楷书（简体）为了写得快，变成"马"。 "马" likes a horse standing upright seen from the side in oracle bone script and bronze script, stressing its eyes and horsehair. Its eyes and horsehair are connected in small seal script. To write faster, it becomes "马" in regular script character (simplified form).	㇆ 马 马

马	mǎ	horse	马虎	mǎhu	careless
马上	mǎshàng	at once	马路	mǎlù	road

以马为意符的字 Characters with "马" to signify meaning	意符在下：驾 意符在左：骑
以马为声符的字 Characters with "马" to signify pronunciation	声符在右：吗 ma　妈 mā

	金文1 Bronze inscriptions 1	金文2 Bronze inscriptions 2	小篆 Small seal script	毛 máo 楷书 Regular script

"毛"，从金文的形体看，象弯弯曲曲的毛发之形。小篆形体与金文接近。楷书的笔画由小篆演变而来，笔画由圆滑变得横直 。"毛"的本义指动植物的皮上所附物、人的毛发及鸟的羽毛。

The ancient form of "毛" is a pictograph of the hair of man or beast. It skillfully smoothens itself and finally straightens into new form "毛". "毛" originally means the hair of man or beast and the feather of bird.

丿 ⺁ 三 毛

毛病	máobìng	shortcomings/fault
毛衣	máoyī	sweater
毛巾	máojīn	towel
羽毛球	yǔmáoqiú	badminton

这台机器又出现了同样的毛病。

Zhè tái jīqì yòu chūxiàn le tóngyàng de máobìng.

The machine appeared the same fault again.

以毛为意符的字 Characters with "毛" to signify meaning	意符在下：笔
小提示 Tips	由"毛"组成的字，大多与毛发有关。 Characters with "毛" are mostly associated with hair or feather.

<table>
<tr><td rowspan="2"></td><td>[小篆 form of 麼]</td><td>麼</td><td>么 me
ma</td></tr>
<tr><td>小篆
Small
seal script</td><td>楷书（繁体）
Regular script
（complex form）</td><td>楷书（简体）
Regular script
（simplified form）</td></tr>
<tr><td colspan="3">“么”，在古代汉语中，与“幺”读音相同，均表示“细小”的意思。后来，繁体字“麼”简化，将“么”作为“麼”的简化字。
In ancient Chinese, “么” and “幺” are homonyms and both mean small. Later, “麼” is simplified to be “么”, which means “么” is the simplified form of “麼” and it no longer means small in modern Chinese.</td><td>丿 么 么</td></tr>
<tr><td colspan="2">多么 duōme how（wonderful, etc.）
那么 nàme so（much）/ like that
这么 zhème so（much）/ like this
什么 shénme what
怎么 zěnme
（interrogative pronoun）/how
为什么 wèishénme why
怎么样 zěnmeyàng how about</td><td colspan="2">没什么 méishénme
（idiom）never mind/nothing
什么的 shénmede and so on</td></tr>
<tr><td>小提示
Tips</td><td colspan="3">“么”有两种读音：“me”和“ma”。一般情况下读“me”，例如上面列出的词组；当放在句尾作疑问助词时读“ma”，例如：你找我有事么（ma）？
“么” has two readings: “me” and “ma”. It usually reads “me”, but when used as a particle at the end of a sentence to form an interrogative, it should be pronounced “ma”.</td></tr>
</table>

甲骨文 Oracle bone script	小篆 Small seal script	楷书（繁体） Regular script (complex form)	楷书（简体） Regular script (simplified form)
		門	门 mén

"门"，甲骨文指两扇对开的大门。小篆、楷书（繁体）字形相近。楷书（简体）为了书写快捷，成了三画。

The character "门" is in the shape of two opposite doors in oracle bone script. Small seal script character is similar to regular script character (complex form). With the result of greater convenience in writing, regular script character (simplified form) "门" turned into three strokes.

丶 丨 门

门	mén	door	部门	bùmén	department
门口	ménkǒu	doorway	专门	zhuānmén	specially

以门为意符的字 Characters with "门" to signify meaning	意符在外：间　问
以门为声符的字 Characters with "门" to signify pronunciation	声符在右：们　mén

甲骨文 Oracle bone script	小篆 Small seal script	楷书 Regular script
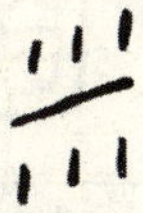		米 mǐ

"米"，甲骨文中，象米粒琐碎散落之形，故"米"的本义指"去壳后粮食作物的子实"，后多指"稻米"。

The earliest form of "米" is a pictograph of rice grains scattering over the ground. So "米" originally means "the grains, seeds or beans of crops". Later it is often used to indicate rice.

丶丷䒑半米米

米	mǐ	rice
米饭	mǐfàn	(cooked) rice
大米	dàmǐ	rice
玉米	yùmǐ	corn
厘米	límǐ	cm (centimeter)

以米为意符的字
Characters with "米" to signify meaning

意符在左：精　糖

小提示
Tips

由"米"组成的字，大多与米或粮食有关。
The characters taking "米" as radicals mostly refer to food.

	甲骨文 1 Oracle bone script 1	甲骨文 2 Oracle bone script 2	小篆 Small seal script	面 miàn 楷书 Regular script

"面"，甲骨文中，中间是一只眼睛，外部是面部轮廓，因五官中眼睛最引人注目，故用眼睛来指明是人的面部。小篆中，中间的眼睛演变为"首"。

The written form of "面" in oracle bone script is like an eye surrounded by frame, which symbols for face. As eyes dominate the whole face, they are highlighted. In small seal script, "目" symbolizing eye becomes "首" symbolizing head erroneously .

方面	fāngmiàn	aspect/side
见面	jiànmiàn	meet
面包	miànbāo	bread
面条	miàntiáo	noodle
北面	běimiàn	northern side
东面	dōngmiàn	eastern side
表面	biǎomiàn	surface
地面	dìmiàn	floor / ground
里面	lǐmiàn	inside
外面	wàimiàn	outside
上面	shàngmiàn	above
下面	xiàmiàn	under/below
片面	piànmiàn	one-sided
全面	quánmiàn	overall
前面	qiánmiàn	front
后面	hòumiàn	back/behind
对面	duìmiàn	opposite
面积	miànjī	area
面貌	miànmào	appearance
面前	miànqián	in front of

小提示 Tips

"面"里边的两竖与上下两横相接，两竖之间是两短横。

The two short vertical strokes inside the square link up with the upper and lower horizontal strokes. Between the two verticals are two parallel short horizontal strokes.

				民 mín
	甲骨文 Oracle bone script	金文 Bronze inscriptions	小篆 Small seal script	楷书 Regular script

“民”，甲骨文和金文中，象用利器刺瞎眼睛之形，表示将人的一只眼睛刺瞎以做奴隶之意，故“民”最初的意义指“奴隶”，后来渐渐指“人”、“人类”。
The written form of “民” in oracle bone script and bronze inscriptions is like piercing knife into an eye of a man to turn him into a slave. So “民” originally means “slaves”, later is extended to indicate “human beings”.

民主	mínzhǔ	democracy	民族	mínzú	ethnic group
国民党	guómíndǎng	the Kuomintang	农民	nóngmín	peasant
人民币	rénmínbì	Renminbi (RMB)	人民	rénmín	people

小提示 Tips	在古代，“人”通常指身份尊贵的人，“民”通常指庶民或奴隶，“人”和“民”的意义不同；在现代汉语中，“人”和“民”连在一起，变成双音节词“人民”，指普通老百姓。 In ancient times, “人” refers to ruler while “民” indicates being ruled. In modern Chinese, “人” and “民” are put together to be a new word “人民”, which means citizens.

					母 mǔ
	甲骨文 Oracle bone script	金文 Bronze inscriptions	小篆 Small seal script	隶书 Clerical script	楷书 Regular script

“母”，甲骨文和金文中，像女子双手交叉、侧身跽坐，并且突出了胸前的两乳。小篆中，双手、乳头拉长，字形发生变化。到了楷书，将“母”的字形逆时针转了90度，身体拉直为一横，成为现在的字形。

The written form of “母” is in the shape of a woman sitting sideways with arms across her breast. Two nipples are highlighted, which means she is the mother of a baby. In small seal script, the stokes of “母” symbolizing nipples and arms are lengthened. “母” in regular script is rotated 90 degrees counterclockwise, and becomes the modern written form.

伯母 bómǔ aunt	母亲 mǔqīn mother

以母为意符的字 Characters with “母” to signify meaning	意符在下：每
小提示 Tips	“母”的第一笔竖折和第二笔横折钩中的竖笔部分都需稍稍向右下倾斜。 The first stroke of “母”, a vertical turning, should slant to the lowcr right slightly. The second stroke, a horizontal turning with a hook, should slant at the same side.

甲骨文 Oracle bone script	金文 Bronze inscriptions	小篆 Small seal script	楷书 Regular script
			目 mù

"目"，甲骨文和金文中，像人的眼睛。小篆中，笔画变得规整圆滑，字形逆时针旋转了 90 度。楷书中，笔画拉直，成为现在的字形。

The written form of "目" in oracle bone script and bronze inscriptions looks like a human eye. It is rotated 90 degrees counterclockwise in small seal script, and to be modern written form.

丨 冂 冃 月 目

节目	jiémù	program/item
目前	mùqián	currently
目标	mùbiāo	target/goal
目的	mùdì	aim/purpose
题目	tímù	subject/topic
项目	xiàngmù	project

以目为意符的字
Characters with "目" to signify meaning

意符在左：睛　睡　眼
意符在下：看　冒　省
意符在右：相

小提示
Tips

有"目"的汉字，一般与眼睛有关，如上面所列举的：睛、眼、看、省、相、睡、冒。

The characters taking "目" as a radical usually refer to eyes, such as the above mentioned characters "睛", "眼", "看", "省", "相", "睡" and "冒".

	甲骨文 Oracle bone script	金文 Bronze inscriptions	小篆 Small seal script	南 nán 楷书 Regular script

"南"，甲骨文和金文字形像一种敲打乐器，小篆字形与金文非常接近。古代乐器都是面朝南陈列，"南"后来表示方位是记音，与"北"相对。

The earliest form of "南" is a pictograph of a musical instrument. In ancient times, musical instruments were always placed facing south. Then "南" is used to indicate the direction of south, the opposite of north.

南边	nánbiān	south
东南	dōngnán	southeast
南部	nánbù	southern part
南方	nánfāng	south
南面	nánmiàn	in the south
西南	xīnán	southwest

小提示 Tips

"南"的第五笔是点，第六笔是短撇，最后一竖与第七笔横相接。

The fifth stroke of "南" is a dot, and the sixth is a left-falling short stroke. Its final vertical links with the seventh horizontal stroke.

<table>
<tr><td rowspan="2"></td><td>(bronze form)</td><td>(seal form)</td><td>(clerical form)</td><td>牛 niú</td></tr>
<tr><td>金文
Bronze inscriptions</td><td>小篆
Small seal script</td><td>隶书
Clerical script</td><td>楷书
Regular script</td></tr>
<tr><td colspan="4">“牛”，金文是正面牛头形，突出向内弯的角。小篆变化不大。隶书省略了牛的右角，变为楷书“牛”。
The character “牛” is in the shape of the head of an ox in bronze inscriptions, stressing its inflexed horns. Small seal script character is similar to bronze inscriptions. Clerical script leaves out its right horn, thus the regular script character “牛” comes into being.</td><td>丿 𠂉 𠂒 牛</td></tr>
<tr><td colspan="2">牛 niú ox
牛奶 niúnǎi milk</td><td colspan="3">我正在煮牛奶。
Wǒ zhèngzài zhǔ niúnǎi.
I am boiling the milk.</td></tr>
<tr><td>以牛为意符的字
Characters with “牛” to signify meaning</td><td colspan="4">意符在右：件　解
意符在左：特　物</td></tr>
</table>

甲骨文 Oracle bone script	金文 Bronze inscriptions	小篆 Small seal script	隶书 Clerical script	女 nǚ 楷书 Regular script

"女"，甲骨文象侧身跽坐的女人之形。金文将弯曲的下肢前伸。小篆将左臂拉长至地。经过隶书变化，成为今文。

The oracle bone script character "女" likes a woman who goes down on her knees. And the bronze inscriptions extends her curving lower limbs forward. The small seal script extends her left arm to the ground. After the evolution of clerical script , the modern character came into being.

女	nǚ	woman
女儿	nǚ'ér	daughter
女人	nǚrén	woman
女士	nǚshì	lady
妇女	fùnǚ	woman

以女为意符的字 Characters with "女" to signify meaning	
意符在下：	安　矮　宴　要
意符在左：	姑　好　姐　妈　妹　奶　娘　如　始　她　姓　努

	甲骨文 1 Oracle bone script 1	甲骨文 2 Oracle bone script 2	小篆 Small seal script	片 piàn 楷书 Regular script
“片”，甲骨文字形像纵向锯开的树木，所以本义指“剖开”或“分开”。因为从中剖开的树木既扁又平，后来“片”经常指一些扁平之物，如“木片”、“名片”等。现在通常用作量词，如“两片面包”、“几片云”等。 The earliest form of “片” is a pictograph of a tree split in the middle, so it originally means “to split something”. As the cleft tree is flat, “片” is used to represent flat things such as “木片”（wood chip）or “名片”（business card）. Now it is often used as a measure word, such as “两片面包”（two pieces of bread）or “几片云”（several clouds）.				丿 丿' 片 片

底片	dǐpiàn	photographic plate	胶片	jiāopiàn	（photographic）film
影片	yǐngpiàn	film/movie	卡片	kǎpiàn	card
明信片	míngxìnpiàn	postcard	图片	túpiàn	picture
			片刻	piànkè	short period of time
			鸦片	yāpiàn	opium

小提示 Tips	“片”的最后一笔是横折，不能错写为两笔。 The final stroke of “片” is a horizontal turning without being broken.

金文 1 Bronze inscriptions 1	金文 2 Bronze inscriptions 2	小篆 Small seal script	隶书 Clerical script	楷书 Regular script
				平 píng

"平"，金文象天平之形，故"平"的本义指"天平"。后引申有地面平坦、心情宁静等意思。

The ancient form of "平" is a pictograph of a balance, so it originally means balance. By extension, "平" is used to express the flat ground or well-balanced heart.

水平 shuǐpíng level

不平	bùpíng	uneven/injustice/disaffection
和平	hépíng	peace
平安	píng'ān	safe and sound
平常	píngcháng	ordinary/ordinarily
平等	píngděng	equality
平方	píngfāng	square
平静	píngjìng	calm
平均	píngjūn	average
平时	píngshí	at ordinary times
平原	píngyuán	plain

以平为声符的字 Characters with "平" to signify pronunciation	声符在下：苹 píng 声符在右：评 píng
小提示 Tips	在现代汉语中，"平"主要表示"平坦"、"平安"、"平常"等意思。 In modern Chinese, "平" usually means flat, safe or ordinary.

<table>
<tr><td rowspan="2"></td><td>(ancient form)</td><td>(ancient form)</td><td>(ancient form)</td><td>七 qī</td></tr>
<tr><td>甲骨文
Oracle
bone script</td><td>金文
Bronze
inscriptions</td><td>小篆
Small
seal script</td><td>楷书
Regular script</td></tr>
<tr><td colspan="4">“七”，甲骨文和金文字形相同，一横一竖交叉。“七”的本义指“切”，一竖代表将一横切断、一分为二。后来作数词“七”，是记音。
The earliest form of “七” is a cross that the horizontal cuts off the vertical or in a reverse order. Therefore, “七” originally means “cut off”, later it is used to indicate seven.</td><td>一七</td></tr>
<tr><td colspan="2">乱七八糟　luànqībāzāo
be in a muddle or a mess
七嘴八舌　qīzuǐbāshé
everybody talking at the same time</td><td colspan="3">房间里乱七八糟的。
Fángjiān lǐ luànqībāzāo de.
The room is in dreadful disorder.</td></tr>
<tr><td>小提示
Tips</td><td colspan="4">“七”在书写时，第一笔是横且稍微向上倾斜。第二笔竖弯钩向右拐弯，不是向左拐弯。
The horizontal stroke of “七” slightly slants to the left. Its vertical upward turning does not turn left but right.</td></tr>
</table>

				齊	齐 qí
	甲骨文 Oracle bone script	金文 Bronze inscriptions	小篆 Small seal script	楷书（繁体） Regular script （complex form）	楷书（简体） Regular script （simplified form）

“齐”，甲骨文和金文字形，像禾麦出穗，全都饱满，没有干瘪的。所以“齐”引申有“齐全”、“整齐”、“一致”等意义。

The earliest form of “齐” is a pictograph of wheat in the ear. The ears all are full and plump, therefore “齐” extends to mean “fully”, “orderly” or “completely”.

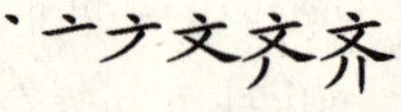

整齐 zhěngqí in good order/orderly	一齐 yīqí all of a lump

小提示 Tips	“齐”的繁体字字形是“齊”。 The original complex form of “齐” is “齊”.

	甲骨文 Oracle bone script	金文 Bronze inscriptions	小篆 Small seal script	其 qí 楷书 Regular script

"其"，甲骨文中象簸箕之形，金文形体加了表示几案的部件，小篆字形加上了表示其材料的"竹"。"其"用作语气词是记音；并且不再表示"簸箕"之义。

The earliest form of "其" is a pictograph of a dustpan. Later people added component (a table) to it, and then added "竹" (indicating "其" is made of bamboo) to it. Therefore, a new character "箕" is produced to indicate dustpan, "其" is used as a mood particle.

一 十 卄 卄 甘
甘 其 其

尤其 yóuqí especially	圣诞节是个快乐的日子，尤其是对孩子们来说。 Shèngdànjié shì gè kuàilè de rìzi, yóuqí shì duì háizimen lái shuō. Christmas is a time of mirth, especially for children.

小提示 Tips	在现代汉语中，"其"通常用作代词，如"自圆其说"；也经常用在词尾，如"尤其"、"极其"等。 In modern Chinese, "其" is usually used as a pronoun, such as "自圆其说"; it is often put in the end of a word, such as "尤其" or "极其".

	三	气	氣	气 qì
	甲骨文 Oracle bone script	金文 Bronze inscriptions	小篆 Small seal script	楷书 Regular script

"气"，甲骨文中以三横表示，像天上云气飘拂的样子。金文中，第一横向上翘而第三横向下拖，渐渐接近现代汉字字形。"气"的本义指"云气"，后引申指一切气体。

The earliest form of "气" is made up of three lines, which represent floating clouds in the sky. Later in order to distinguish from "三" (three), the direction of the upper line turns up, and the lower line turns down. Originally "气" means floating clouds, then it is extended to mean everything in the gaseous state.

ノ 𠂉 气 气

客气	kèqì	courteous/polite
空气	kōngqì	air
天气	tiānqì	weather
力气	lìqì	strength
煤气	méiqì	coal gas
暖气	nuǎnqì	heater
脾气	píqì	temperament
气候	qìhòu	climate
气温	qìwēn	air temperature
气象	qìxiàng	weather
生气	shēngqì	get angry
勇气	yǒngqì	courage
语气	yǔqì	tone

以气为声符的字 Characters with "气" to signify pronunciation	声符在右：汽 qì
小提示 Tips	"气"的繁体字字形是"氣"。 The original complex form of "气" is "氣".

<table>
<tr><td rowspan="2"></td><td></td><td></td><td></td><td>千 qiān</td></tr>
<tr><td>甲骨文
Oracle
bone script</td><td>金文
Bronze
inscriptions</td><td>小篆
Small
seal script</td><td>楷书
Regular script</td></tr>
<tr><td colspan="4">“千”，甲骨文和金文字形像向左侧立的人，下面加了一横，与“人”相区别，表数目“一千”。
The earliest form of “千” is in the shape of a man standing sideways with a horizontal crossed his leg, which is used to distinguish “千” from “人”. “千” originally means one thousand.</td><td>㇒ 二 千</td></tr>
<tr><td colspan="2">千万 qiānwàn ten million
be sure to/must</td><td colspan="3">这家乡镇企业固定资产达千万。
Zhèjiā xiāngzhèn qǐyè gùdìngzīchǎn dá qiānwàn.
The fixed assets of this township enterprise now stand at 10 million yuan in value.
我们千万不能那样做。
Wǒmen qiānwàn bùnéng nàyàng zuò.
We absolutely can't do that.</td></tr>
<tr><td>小提示
Tips</td><td colspan="4">注意区别“千”与“干”，“千”的上部是一撇，而“干”的上部是一横。
It should be noted that the first stroke of “千” is a left-falling stroke while the one of “干” is a horizontal stroke.</td></tr>
</table>

甲骨文 Oracle bone script	金文 Bronze inscriptions	小篆 Small seal script	且 qiě 楷书 Regular script

"且"，从甲骨文、金文、小篆到楷书，字形没有显著变化，像男性生殖器的形状，象征男性，所以"且"在甲骨、金文中常用来指男性祖先。

The written form of "且" from ancient to modern times doesn't have observably change. It looks like the male reproductive organ, which is the symbol for male ancestor in oracle bone script.

而且 érqiě moreover	并且 bìngqiě and/besides

以且为意符的字 Characters with "且" to signify meaning	意符在右：祖
小提示 Tips	"且"在甲骨、金文中指男性祖先，但在现代汉字中通常用作连词，表示"尚且"、"并且"等意义。 "且" means male ancestors in ancient, while it is always used as conjunction meaning "even" or "and" in modern.

			親	亲 qīn
	金文 Bronze inscriptions	小篆 Small seal script	楷书（繁体） Regular script (complex form)	楷书（简体） Regular script (simplified form)

“亲”的繁体字字形由“辛”、“木”、“見”组合而成。“辛”在古文字中指“刀”，用刀砍下“木”，制成牌位恭拜，就是“亲”。因祖庙中摆列的牌位多为父母的，“亲”有了“父亲”、“母亲”之义。后又引申有“亲属”、“亲密”之义。

The original complex form of “亲” is an ideograph, made up of “辛”, “木”, and “見”. In ancient times, “辛” represented knife, and “木” indicated wood. The three components are put together to mean cutting wood to make shrine. As shrines in ancestral temple were always belong to parents', therefore “亲” was used to indicate parents. By extension, “亲” means “relatives” and “close or intimate”.

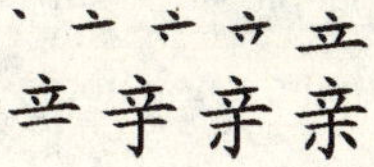

父亲	fùqīn	father
母亲	mǔqīn	mother
亲爱	qīn'ài	dear
亲戚	qīn · qi	relative/kin
亲切	qīnqiè	friendly
亲自	qīnzì	in person

小提示 Tips

“亲”的繁体字字形是“親”。

The original complex form of “亲” is “親”.

<table>
<tr><td rowspan="2"></td><td></td><td></td><td></td><td>求 qiú</td></tr>
<tr><td>甲骨文
Oracle
bone script</td><td>金文
Bronze
inscriptions</td><td>小篆
Small
seal script</td><td>楷书
Regular script</td></tr>
<tr><td colspan="4">“求”，甲骨文字形像毛皮外露的衣服，故指皮衣。金文和小篆字形，中间多了表示兽皮的部件，成为“裘”。于是，本身指“皮衣”的“求”就用来表示“寻求”、“追求”、“请求”等意义。
The form of “求” in oracle bone is a pictograph of a fur coat. Later people added a component, which resembled skin of animal, to produce a new form “裘”. Therefore, “求” originally means “fur coat”, is used to indicate “seek”, “pursue” or “request”.</td><td>一 寸 寸 才 氺 求 求</td></tr>
<tr><td colspan="2">要求 yāoqiú require/demand</td><td colspan="3">请求 qǐngqiú request
征求 zhēngqiú solicit/ask for
实事求是 shishiqiúshi realistic</td></tr>
<tr><td>以求为声符的字
Characters with “求” to signify pronunciation</td><td colspan="4">声符在右：球 qiú</td></tr>
<tr><td>小提示
Tips</td><td colspan="4">“求”的第三笔是点，第四笔是提，书写时两笔不能连在一起。
The third stroke of “求” is a dot, and the fourth stroke begins from the lower left to the upward right. The two strokes are not supposed to be connected.</td></tr>
</table>

	甲骨文 Oracle bone script	小篆 Small seal script	隶书 Clerical script	楷书 Regular script
				人 rén

"人"，甲骨文像侧身而立的人。小篆虽躬身提臀，仍然不失人形。经过隶书变化，成为今文。

The oracle bone script character "人" looks like someone standing on his side. The small seal script character looks like someone bowing with his buttock lifted. After the evolution of clerical script, the modern character comes into being.

丿 人

人	rén	people
人们	rénmen	people
人民	rénmín	the people
爱人	àirén	spouse
别人	biérén	other people
夫人	fūrén	madam
工人	gōngrén	worker
人才	réncái	a talented person
人员	rényuán	staff
病人	bìngrén	patient
大人	dàrén	adult
敌人	dírén	enemy
客人	kèrén	guest
老人	lǎorén	the aged
男人	nánrén	man
女人	nǚrén	woman
主人	zhǔrén	host

以人为意符的字
Characters with "人" to signify meaning

意符在上或在右，写成"人"：介 从 以

意符在左，写成"亻"：便 代 但 倒 低 傅 何 候 化 假 件 健 借 例 们 你 任 什 使 他 体 停 位 像 信 休 亿 住 做 作

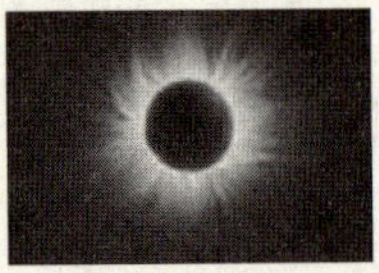				日 rì
	金文 Bronze inscriptions	甲骨文 Oracle bone script	小篆 Small seal script	楷书 Regular script

"日"即太阳。金文在圆环中加一点，有学者指出，一点是指太阳黑子。如果真如此，那中国古人对太阳的认识就十分先进了。甲骨文呈方形，是因为刀刻不便。小篆、楷书变化不大。

The character "日" represents the sun. The bronze inscriptions adds a dot to the circle. The oracle bone script character is square , due to the difficulty of engraving the hard, bony surfaces by knives. The character is similar in small seal script , regular script and oracle bone script .

丨 冂 月 日

日	rì	day	日常	rìcháng	daily
日语	rìyǔ	Japanese	日程	rìchéng	agenda
日文	rìwén	Japanese	日记	rìjì	diary
日子	rì · zi	day	日期	rìqī	date
节日	jiérì	festival	日用品	rìyòngpǐn	articles of everyday use
生日	shēngrì	birthday	日元	rìyuán	YEN
星期日	xīngqīrì	Sunday	礼拜日	lǐbàirì	Sunday

以日为意符的字 Characters with "日" to signify meaning	意符在上中下：早 但 是 提 题 晨 星 影 宴 间 简 朝 借 春 意符在左右：明 暖 时 晴 晚 昨 旧 照
小提示 Tips	日 rì：狭长一点。 曰 yuē：扁宽一点。 The character "日"（rì）is a little long and narrow . The character "曰"（yuē）is some of flat.

				肉 ròu
	甲骨文 Oracle bone script	金文 Bronze inscriptions	汉简 Han bamboo script	楷书 Regular script

"肉"，甲骨文、金文像一块供食用的动物肉。经过汉简演变，就成了楷书的"肉"。 Both oracle bone script and bronze inscriptions of the character "肉" (meat) look like a piece of meat we eat. After the evolution of han bamboo script, it turned into regular script character "肉".	丨冂内内肉肉
肉　ròu　meat	
以肉为意符的字 Characters with "肉" to signify meaning	意符在下：有　育 意符在左右：脚　脸　脏　脆　脱　湖 意符在左上：然
小提示 Tips	"湖"、"脚"、"脸"、"脏"等：其中的"月"是"肉"(ròu)变来的。 "月" in characters such as "湖", "脚", "脸" and "脏", is transformed from character "肉" (meat). "明"、"望"、"朝"、"期"等：其中的"月"(yuè)是月亮变来的。参见"月"字。 "月" in characters such as "明", "望", "朝" and "期" is transformed from character "月" (the moon). "服"、"胜"等：其中的"月"是"舟"(zhōu)变来的。参见"服"字。 "月" in characters such as "服" and "胜" is transformed from character "舟" (boat).

				三 sān
	甲骨文 Oracle bone script	金文 Bronze inscriptions	小篆 Small seal script	楷书 Regular script

“三”，甲骨文、金文和小篆的字形都相同，画等长的三横表示数字“三”。楷书字形有细微差别，中间一横最短，上面一横比下面一横稍短。“三”最初也是记数符号，后经常用来指“多数”、“多次”等意义。 In ancient times, people drown three equilong horizontals to represent three. The three lines of regular form aren’t equilong that the upper line is shorter than lower, and the middle is the shortest. By extension, “三” is often used to mean “numerous” or “multiple”.	一 二 三

再三 zàisān again and again	三角 sānjiǎo a triangle 接二连三 jiē’èrliánsān one after the other 三番五次 sānfānwǔcì time and again 朝三暮四 zhāosānmùsì play fast and loose

小提示 Tips	“三”在书写时，第二横最短，第三横最长。三横之间的距离差不多相等。 Of the three horizontal strokes the second one is the shortest, and the third one is the longest. The space between each stroke is almost the same.

甲骨文 Oracle bone script	金文 Bronze inscriptions	小篆 Small seal script	楷书 Regular script
			山 shān

"山"，甲骨文和金文中，象山峰并立之形。三个山峰表示多数，即群峰起伏之状。

The earliest form of "山" is a pictograph of three mountain peaks. In ancient times, people tended to use three as a lot, so "山" was more than three peaks.

山脉 shānmài mountain chain
山区 shānqū a mountainous area

喜马拉雅山脉绵延数千公里。
Xǐmǎlāyǎ shānmài miányán shù qiān gōnglǐ.
The Himalayas stretches for thousands of kilometers.

他来自一个贫困山区。
Tā láizì yīgè pínkùn shānqū.
He comes from a poverty mountain village.

小提示 Tips

由"山"组成的字，大多与山岭有关。
The characters with "山" as radicals mostly refer to mountain.

	二	二	丄	上 shàng
	甲骨文 Oracle bone script	金文 Bronze inscriptions	小篆 Small seal script	楷书 Regular script

"上"，甲骨文和金文字形相同，下面一长横表示地面，上面一短横是指事符号，表示地面之上。小篆字形加了一竖，楷书字形将一竖拉直，成为现代字形。

Above and below are relative and abstract terms, man conveyed the ideas graphically by relating a simple stroke to a horizontal foundation line "一". This stroke above base line was originally a short line "二", embellished and finally stabilized "上".

丨 ⺊ 上

马上	mǎshàng	immediately	路上	lù · shang	on the way
上边	shàng · bian	above	上班	shàngbān	go to work
上课	shàngkè	give lessons	上当	shàngdàng	be caught with chaff
上来	shànglái	come up	上级	shàngjí	superior
上去	shàngqù	go up	上面	shàngmiàn	above
上午	shàngwǔ	morning	上衣	shàngyī	upper outer garment
上学	shàngxué	go to school	以上	yǐshàng	more than/over/above
晚上	wǎn · shang	night			
早上	zǎo · shang	morning	之上	zhīshàng	above

小提示 Tips	"上"在书写时，上横在竖笔的右边，与竖相接。 The short horizontal of "上" is connected with the vertical on the right.

	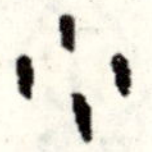	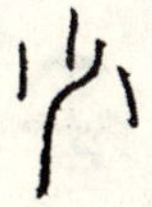	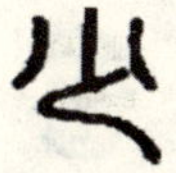	少 shǎo shào
	甲骨文 Oracle bone script	金文 Bronze inscriptions	小篆 Small seal script	楷书 Regular script

"少"，甲骨文字形是画四个小点，表示不多。金文字形中将左右两小点拉长了，小篆字形将下面一小点艺术化处理了，楷书又将之变为一撇。

The concept of few or small is clarified in relation to sands or other tiny things, man conveyed ideas graphically by putting four dots together. Later the two dots on right and left were straightened, then embellished and finally stabilized "少".

丨 ⺌ 小 少

多少	duō · shao	how many/ how much
	duōshǎo	somewhat
不少	bùshǎo	quit a few
减少	jiǎnshǎo	reduce
缺少	quēshǎo	be short of
少数	shǎoshù	fewness
至少	zhìshǎo	at least
少年	shàonián	early youth

小提示 Tips

"少"有两个读音"shǎo"和"shào". 表示数量小（跟"多"相对）或缺少（跟"多"相对）时，读作"shǎo"；表示年纪轻（跟"老"相对），读作"shào"。

"少" has two different readings. When it indicates small quantity or be short of, it should be pronounced as "shǎo"; when it is used to express young, it reads "shào".

				舍 shě shè
	金文 1 Bronze inscriptions 1	金文 2 Bronze inscriptions 2	小篆 Small seal script	楷书 Regular script

“舍”，金文字形的上部“人”像屋顶，中间部分的“干”像屋里的顶柱和横梁，下部的“口”像用砖石砌的墙基。所以，“舍”的本义指“房屋”。

“舍” is made up of three parts. The upper part is a pictograph of housetop, the middle part indicates the shore and cross beam, and the lower part represents the footing of wall. So “舍” originally means house.

宿舍 sùshè dormitory	他住在学校的宿舍里。 Tā zhùzài xuéxiào de sùshè lǐ. He lives in the school dormitory.
小提示 Tips	“舍”有两种读音：作名词指房屋时，读作“shè”，如“宿舍”等；作动词指舍弃时，读作“shě”，如“四舍五入”等。 “舍” has two different readings. When it refers to house, it should be pronounced as “shè”, such as “宿舍 ” (sùshè); when it is used as a verb to mean “give up”, it reads “shě”, for example, “四舍五入 ” (sì shě wǔ rù).

				身 shēn
	甲骨文 Oracle bone script	金文 Bronze inscriptions	小篆 Small seal script	楷书 Regular script
“身”，甲骨文和金文中，象人侧面而立、腹部隆起，即怀有身孕之形，所以本义指身孕。小篆中，人的形体有所变化，但腹部凸起之形仍可看出。楷书中，笔画拉直。 The written form of “身” in oracle bone script and bronze inscriptions is in the shape of a pregnant woman standing sideways, therefore it means pregnant originally. Its written form is changed in small seal script while the distend belly is still visible. The strokes are straightened in regular script.				′ 亻 ㄏ 月 自 身 身
身体 shēntǐ body		动身 dòngshēn leave/go on a journey 身边 shēnbiān at one's side		
以身为意符的字 Characters with “身” to signify meaning	意符在左：躺			
小提示 Tips	“身”在甲骨文、金文中指有身孕，但在现代汉字中通常用来表示“身体”、“生命”等意义。 “身” means pregnant in ancient times, while it always means body or life in modern.			

甲骨文 Oracle bone script	金文 Bronze inscriptions	小篆 Small seal script	生 shēng 楷书 Regular script

“生”，甲骨文和金文中，像草木破土而出、生根发芽的形态，下面一横即代表地面。所以“生”的本义指“草木长出、生长”，后引申有“生育”、“生长”、“生产”等意义。

The earliest form of “生” is an ideograph. The lower horizontal “一” stands for the ground, and the upper part is like a new growth of grass. So originally “生” means “grass breaks through from soil”, later it is extended to mean “bear”, “grow” or “produce”.

丿 𠂉 𠂒 牛 生

发生	fāshēng	happen
生日	shēngrì	birthday
先生	xiān · sheng	Mr.
生产	shēngchǎn	produce
学生	xuéshēng	student
留学生	liúxuéshēng	student abroad
生词	shēngcí	new word
医生	yīshēng	doctor
生活	shēnghuó	living

我不知道发生了什么事。
Wǒ bùzhīdào fāshēng le shénme shì.
I don't know what happened.

以生为意符的字 Characters with “生” to signify meaning	意符在右：姓
以生为声符的字 Characters with “生” to signify pronunciation	胜 shèng

甲骨文 Oracle bone script	小篆 Small seal script	楷书（繁体） Regular script (complex form)	楷书（简体） Regular script (simplified form)
		聲	声 shēng

"声"，甲骨文字形由五部分组成，左上部是一只磬的形状，右边是一只手拿着小锤敲打磬，磬的下面是一只耳朵和一张口，表示"磬声"入耳。现在，"声"通常指各种响声、人说话的声音或音乐声。

The earliest form of "声" is an ideograph. At the upper left was a pictograph of a big mountain stone, which was beating by a hammer in a hand at the right. Under the stone were an ear and a mouth, which meant "to listen to the sound from stone". Now it usually means all different sounds such as noise, voice or musical sound.

大声	dàshēng	loud
声调	shēngdiào	tone
声音	shēngyīn	sound

别那么大声地说话。
Bié nàme dàshēng de shuōhuà.
Don't talk so loud.

小提示 Tips	"声"的繁体字字形是"聲"。 The original complex form of "声" is "聲".

				十 shí
	甲骨文 Oracle bone script	金文 Bronze inscriptions	小篆 Small seal script	楷书 Regular script

"十"，甲骨文字形像筹码竖置。金文字形中间加了一点，表示结绳记事。小篆中间的一点变为一横，与楷书相同。

The oracle bone script form of "十" is like counter stalled vertically, and later people add a dot in the middle of it, which may be a knot in rope to keep records. Then with a straightening out, man derived the regular form "十".

一十

十分 shífēn very/absolutely	这套毛料套装十分昂贵。 Zhètào máoliào tàozhuāng shífēn ángguì. This wool suit is very expensive.
以十为意符的字 Characters with "十" to signify meaning	意符在下：章 意符在右：什
以十为声符的字 Characters with "十" to signify pronunciation	什 shí

	丅	亍	示	示 shì
	甲骨文 1 Oracle bone script 1	甲骨文 2 Oracle bone script 2	小篆 Small seal script	楷书 Regular script

"示"，甲骨文字形像宗庙中祖先的牌位，小篆字形下部左右各加了一笔。所以，"示"在甲骨文时代通常指天神、祖先等。因古代常举行祭祀活动，请求天神、祖先给予预示，所以"示"后来有"预示"、"给人看"之义。

The earliest form of "示" is a pictograph of a shrine for forefather in ancestral temple, later people add two strokes in right and left to produce the small seal script form. In ancient times, "示" represents gods or ancestors, as people often hold ceremonies to worship heaven to ask for omen, then it extends to mean "foretell" or "show people something".

一 二 亍 亍 示

表示 biǎoshì to show	指示 zhǐshì indicate/instructions

小提示 Tips	"示"作为部首时，通常写作"礻"；由"礻"组成的字，通常与崇拜、祝愿、鬼神、祭祀有关，如：福、祝、神、祀。 As a radical, "示" is usually written as "礻"; characters with "礻" mostly refer to worship, sacrifice, ghosts and gods.

<table>
<tr><td></td><td></td><td></td><td></td><td>世 shì</td></tr>
<tr><td></td><td>金文 1
Bronze
inscriptions 1</td><td>金文 2
Bronze
inscriptions 2</td><td>小篆
Small
seal script</td><td>楷书
Regular script</td></tr>
<tr><td colspan="4">“世”，金文字形象分杈的树枝长出新芽之形，“世”的本义指树枝上长出的树叶。树叶通常茂盛重叠，所以“世”又引申指世世代代。
The written form of “世” in bronze inscriptions is like a tree putting forth new leaves, so it originally means leaves of tree. As leaves look thick, it extends to mean generational.</td><td>一 十 廿 廿 世</td></tr>
</table>

世界 shìjiè world	世纪 shìjì century

小提示 Tips	在现代汉语中，“世”通常指人的一生，如“一世”；或者指一个世代、一百年，如“世纪”；或者指世界。 In modern Chinese, “世” usually indicates lifetime, such as “一世”; or it refers to a century, such as “世纪”; or it means the world, such as “世界”.

<table>
<tr><td rowspan="2"></td><td>(金文1 form)</td><td>(金文2 form)</td><td>(小篆 form)</td><td>手 shǒu</td></tr>
<tr><td>金文1
Bronze inscriptions 1</td><td>金文2
Bronze inscriptions 2</td><td>小篆
Small seal script</td><td>楷书
Regular script</td></tr>
<tr><td colspan="4">“手”，在金文和小篆中，像人手腕以下的指掌部分。在楷书中，表示手指的曲线被拉直，成为现在的字形。
The ancient written form of “手” is like five fingers of a palm. In regular script, the curved strokes of “手” symbolizing fingers are straightened to be horizontal ones.</td><td>一 二 三 手</td></tr>
<tr><td colspan="2">手表 shǒubiǎo watch
握手 wòshǒu to shake hands</td><td colspan="3">动手 dòngshǒu to start work/fight
手段 shǒuduàn method
手工 shǒugōng handwork
手帕 shǒupà handkerchief
手术 shǒushù surgical operation
手套 shǒutào glove
手续 shǒuxù formalities
手指 shǒuzhǐ finger</td></tr>
<tr><td>以手为意符的字
Characters with “手” to signify meaning</td><td colspan="4">意符在下：拿 掌</td></tr>
<tr><td>小提示
Tips</td><td colspan="4">为了书写的方便，“手”作为偏旁在隶书中写作“扌”，并沿用至今；由“扌”组成的汉字，大多与手的动作有关，如：把、搬、抱、打、接、拉、拍、抬、提、推、握、找、指。
In order to write more conveniently, “手” as a radical sometimes is written as “扌” in clerical script which has been retained today, and characters with “扌” mostly refer to actions you have to use your hands, such as the words above.</td></tr>
</table>

				首 shǒu
	甲骨文 Oracle bone script	金文 Bronze inscriptions	小篆 Small seal script	楷书 Regular script

“首”，甲骨文字形简单，像一个兽头。金文字形象人眼睛上部有头发之形，故“首”用来指头。小篆从金文蜕变而来，头顶的三根头发还在。楷书中三根头发已经变为两点了。

The earliest form of “首” is like an animal head. In bronze inscriptions, it looks like a people's eye with few hairs above, so it indicates head. The hairs of “首” are still visible in small seal script while changed to two dots in regular script.

首先 shǒuxiān first	首都 shǒudū capital

以首为意符的字 Characters with “首” to signify meaning	意符在右上角：道
小提示 Tips	“首”的本义指“头”，因为“头”是身体最重要也最引人注意的部分，由此引申有“第一”之义。所以，一个国家的中央政府所在地称为“首都”，第一时间做某事称为“首先”。 The original meaning of “首” is head. As head is thought to be the most important and remarkable part of one's body, it extends to mean top or first.

	朩	𣎳	术 shù
	甲骨文 Oracle bone script	小篆 Small seal script	楷书 Regular script

“术”，在甲骨文字形中，中间像一只手，两侧是手运动的弧线，所以“术”本义指“一种手的技巧”，如“技术”、“巫术”、“武术”等。

The form of “术” in oracle bone script is composed of a moving hand and several curves, so “术” originally means “ a skill by hands”, for example, “technique”, “witchcraft ” and “martial arts”, all of which take advantages of hands.

一 十 才 木 术

技术 jìshù technique/technology
艺术 yìshù art

美术 měishù the fine arts
手术 shǒushù operation/ surgery
武术 wǔshù wushu/ Martial arts
学术 xuéshù academic
技术员 jìshùyuán technician

小提示
Tips

“木”的右上角加一点成为“术”。

The character “术” is written by adding a dot to the upper right part of “木”.

甲骨文 Oracle bone script	金文 Bronze inscriptions	小篆 Small seal script	楷书 Regular script
			束 shù

“束”，在甲骨文中，象在树木上缠绕绳索之形，所以本义为“捆绑”，后来引申有“约束”之义。金文和小篆中，树木上缠绕的绳索变为圆环的形状。

The earliest form of “束” is in the shape of sticks bound together with ropes, therefore originally “束” means “binding” and then extends to mean “control”. Later the form of “束” is changed lightly: the ropes binding sticks are replaced by something like a circle.

结束 jiéshù end/conclude	六点钟不到电影就结束了。 Liùdiǎnzhōng bùdào diànyǐng jiù jiéshù le. The movie was over shortly before six.

以束为声符的字 Characters with “束” to signify pronunciation	声符在中间：漱 shù
小提示 Tips	要注意区分“束”与“朿”，“束”字下面封口，而“朿”字不封口。 Be aware of the difference of “束” and “朿”. The middle part of “束” is closed while “朿” is open.

甲骨文 Oracle bone script	金文 Bronze inscriptions	小篆 Small seal script	汉简 Han bamboo script	楷书 Regular script
				水 shuǐ

"水"，甲骨文和金文中，中间的曲线表示河流，两边的点表示水点，而水点的多少并不固定。

The earliest form of "水" is an ideograph of a river and several water drops. The middle curve stands for a river and the dots represent water drops, the number of which are not fixed.

汽水	qìshuǐ	soft drink
水果	shuǐguǒ	fruit
水平	shuǐpíng	level/standard
墨水	mòshuǐ	writing ink
水稻	shuǐdào	rice
水泥	shuǐní	cement
热水瓶	rèshuǐpíng	vacuum bottle
暖水瓶	nuǎnshuǐpíng	vacuum bottle

以水为意符的字 Characters with "水" to signify meaning	意符在左：海 河 湖 江 酒 渴 流 满 没 漂 汽 浅 清 深 汤 洗 泳 游 澡
小提示 Tips	为了书写的方便，"水"作为偏旁在隶书中写作"氵"，并沿用至今，如上面那些字；由"水"或"氵"组成的字，大多与水有关。 In order to write more conveniently, "水" as a radical sometimes is written as "氵" in clerical script which has been retained today; characters with "水" or "氵" mostly refer to water.

				四 sì
	甲骨文 Oracle bone script	金文 Bronze inscriptions	小篆 Small seal script	楷书 Regular script

“四”，甲骨文和金文初期，画等长的四横表示数字“四”。金文后期的字形则像鼻子出气的样子，这个字形本义指“鼻息”、“气息”，后来作数词“四”是记音。小篆字形又省掉了里面的一横。楷书字形跟小篆相同。

The earliest form of “四” is four equilong lines, later it is replaced by a new character, which is a pictograph of using nose to breathe. Omitting the short horizontal inside, people derived the modern reinforced form “四”.

四处	sìchù	all over the place
四周	sìzhōu	all around
四面八方	sìmiànbāfāng	from far and near
四方	sìfāng	four-way/four-sided
四季	sìjì	the four seasons
四肢	sìzhī	the four limbs of the body
朝三暮四	zhāosānmùsì	play fast and loose

小提示 Tips

“四”在书写时，先写里面的撇和竖弯，最后写下面的横封口。

Write the strokes inside the frame before enclosing it. Namely, the left falling and vertical turning strokes of “四” should be given before the square is closed.

小篆 Small seal script	太 tài 楷书 Regular script
"太"，小篆象成年人正面站立之形，但下部多出一点，在字形上与"大"相别。最初"太"与"大"意义相同，后来"太"有"过于"之义，因此又引申有"最"、"极"等意义。 The written form of "太" is in the shape of a standing man with an added dot below, which is used to distinguish "太" from "大". The meaning of "太" and "大" were same originally, and later "太" meant "excessively", which extended to "most".	一 ナ 大 太

太阳 tàiyáng sun	太太 tàitài Mrs. /Madam 老太太 lǎotàitài old lady

以太为声符的字 Characters with "太" to signify pronunciation	声符在上：态 tài
小提示 Tips	"大"字下面加一点成为"太"。 The character "太" is written by adding a dot to the bottom of "大".

	甲骨文 Oracle bone script	金文 Bronze inscriptions	小篆 Small seal script	天 tiān 楷书 Regular script

"天"，甲骨文和金文中，象人正面站立之形，且突出了人的头部，故"天"的本义指人的额部、脑袋。小篆中，人的头部简化为一横，到了楷书，人的上肢拉直，成为现在的字形。

The earliest form of "天" is in the shape of a standing man with his head highlighted, so it originally means people's head, which is simplified to a horizontal bar in small seal script, and the man's hands are stretched in regular script.

一 二 于 天

半天	bàntiān	half of the day			
春天	chūntiān	spring			
夏天	xiàtiān	summer	白天	báitiān	daytime
秋天	qiūtiān	autumn/fall	前天	qiántiān	the day before yesterday
冬天	dōngtiān	winter	后天	hòutiān	the day after tomorrow
今天	jīntiān	today	聊天	liáotiān	chat/talk
明天	míngtiān	tomorrow	天真	tiānzhēn	innocent/ naive
昨天	zuótiān	yesterday	礼拜天	lǐbàitiān	Sunday
天气	tiānqì	weather			
星期天	xīngqītiān	Sunday			

小提示 Tips	"大"字上面加一横成为"天"。 The character "天" is written by adding a horizontal stroke to the top of "大".

<table>
<tr><td rowspan="2"></td><td></td><td></td><td></td><td>万 wàn</td></tr>
<tr><td>甲骨文
Oracle
bone script</td><td>金文
Bronze
inscriptions</td><td>小篆
Small
seal script</td><td>楷书
Regular script</td></tr>
<tr><td colspan="4">“万”，甲骨文和金文中，象蝎子之形。所以本义指“蝎子”，后来作数词是记音，指“千的十倍”。
The earliest form of “万” is a pictograph of a scorpion, so “万” originally means scorpion. Later it is used to express “ten thousand”.</td><td>一 丆 万</td></tr>
<tr><td colspan="2">千万 qiānwàn　ten million</td><td colspan="3">这家乡镇企业固定资产达千万。
Zhèjiā xiāngzhèn qǐyè gùdìng zīchǎn dá qiānwàn.
The fixed assets of this township enterprise now stand at 10 million yuan in value.
我们千万不能那样做。
Wǒmen qiānwàn bùnéng nàyàng zuò.
We absolutely can’t do that.</td></tr>
<tr><td>小提示
Tips</td><td colspan="4">“万”的繁体字字形是“萬”。
The original complex form of “万” is “萬”.</td></tr>
</table>

	甲骨文 Oracle bone script	金文 Bronze inscriptions	小篆 Small seal script	楷书（繁体） Regular script （complex form）	楷书（简体） Regular script （simplified form）
				為	为 wéi wèi

"为"，甲骨文中，右边部分像一头长鼻子大象，左边部分像人的手。所以"为"的本义是"以手驯象"，后来引申出"制作"、"治理"等意义。

"为" is an ideograph，which is made up of a hand and an elephant. The two components are put together to mean "to train elephant with hands". By extension，it means "make" or "control".

丶 ソ 为 为

认为	rènwéi	think/consider
以为	yǐwéi	suppose
为了	wèile	for/in order to
因为	yīnwèi	because/on account of
为什么	wèishénme	why
成为	chéngwéi	become/turn into
作为	zuòwéi	as/action

小提示 Tips

"为"有两种读音：作动词，表示"制作"、"治理"等意义时，读"wéi"，如"认为"、"以为"、"成为"、"作为"；作介词，表示"给"或"因为"等意义时，读"wèi"，如"为了"、"因为"。

"为" has two different readings. When it is used as a verb to indicate "make"，it should be pronounced as "wéi"，such as "认为"，"以为"，"成为" and "作为"；and when it is a preposition，it is read as "wèi"，for example，"为了" and "因为".

				文 wén
	甲骨文 Oracle bone script	金文 Bronze inscriptions	小篆 Small seal script	楷书 Regular script
"文"，甲骨文和金文中，像人正面站立，胸前画有"丿"、"乂"等各类纹饰，故"文"的本义指在肌肤上刺画花纹。从花纹引申有"文字"之义，后来又引申有"文章"之义。 The earliest form of "文" is in the shape of a standing man with tattoos, such as "丿" or "乂" in chest, so its original meaning is to tattoo in skin, which extends to mean "characters" and "articles".				丶 亠 ナ 文

法文	fǎwén	French			
日文	rìwén	Japanese	德文	déwén	German
英文	yīngwén	English	论文	lùnwén	thesis/paper
中文	zhōngwén	Chinese language	文件	wénjiàn	document/file
课文	kèwén	text	文明	wénmíng	civilization
文化	wénhuà	culture	文物	wénwù	cultural relic
文学	wénxué	literature	文字	wénzì	character
文艺	wényì	literature and art	作文	zuòwén	composition
文章	wénzhāng	article	阿拉伯文	ālābówén	Arabic
文学家	wénxuéjiā	writer			

小提示 Tips	由"文"所组成的汉字，其字义大多与花纹有关，例如：斐、斑。 Characters with "文" mostly refer to tattoos, such as "斐" and "斑".

				我 wǒ
	甲骨文 Oracle bone script	金文 Bronze inscriptions	小篆 Small seal script	楷书 Regular script

“我”，甲骨文和金文中，字形像武器——戈。甲骨文的上部朝左的部分是三锋戈，右边是长柄。金文的右部也可以清楚看出是“戈”形。但是在实际使用中，“我”并不指武器，而是用作第一人称代词，称为记音字。

The earliest form of “我” is a pictograph of a dagger-axe, an ancient Chinese weapon. Now the form of dagger-axe is not used to indicate weapon, but only used as the first person pronoun “I” or “me”.

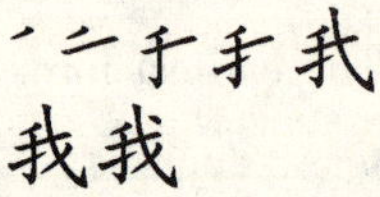

我们 wǒmen we/us	自我 zìwǒ oneself/ego

小提示 Tips

“我”的第四笔是提，不是撇；第五笔斜钩与第二笔横相交，但与第一笔撇不相接。

The fourth stroke of “我” is not a left falling but a rising stroke. The fifth slant hook on its right goes across the second horizontal stroke without connecting with the first left-falling.

<table>
<tr><td rowspan="2"></td><td>㐅</td><td>㐅</td><td>㐅</td><td>五 wǔ</td></tr>
<tr><td>甲骨文
Oracle
bone script</td><td>金文
Bronze
inscriptions</td><td>小篆
Small
seal script</td><td>楷书
Regular script</td></tr>
<tr><td colspan="4">“五”，甲骨文、金文和小篆的字形相同。古人结绳记事，“㐅”像两股绳索交叉的样子，用来表示数字“五”。楷书字形有了较大变化，第三画变为横折。
The ancient form of “五” is a pictograph of two crossed ropes. The ancients kept records by tying knots and five was relatively large, then they used two crossed ropes to represent five. Changing the third stroke to be a horizontal turn, people produced the regular form “五”.</td><td>一 丆 万 五</td></tr>
</table>

三番五次 sānfānwǔcì time and again	我三番五次地告诉过你，不要做那种事。 Wǒ sānfānwǔcì de gàosù guò nǐ, bùyào zuò nàzhǒng shì. I've told you not to do that again and again.
小提示 Tips	“五”在书写时，第二笔和第三笔的竖笔稍微向左下倾斜。 In writing “五” the vertical stroke in the middle and vertical part of the turning should slightly slant to the lower left.

<table>
<tr><td rowspan="2"></td><td></td><td></td><td></td><td>午 wǔ</td></tr>
<tr><td>甲骨文
Oracle
bone script</td><td>金文
Bronze
inscriptions</td><td>小篆
Small
seal script</td><td>楷书
Regular script</td></tr>
<tr><td colspan="4">“午”，甲骨文字形象两头粗、中间细的杵之形。金文字形上部加了左右伸展的把手。所以，“午”的本义指“杵”。现在，“午”通常指时间，即日中的时候，或白天十二点。
The earliest form of “午” is a pictograph of pestle, then people add handles to it. Originally “午” indicates pestle, and now it generally means midday.</td><td>丿 𠂉 二 午</td></tr>
</table>

上午	shàngwǔ	morning	真不幸，上午我的自行车丢了，下午钱包又被偷了！ Zhēn bùxìng, shàngwǔ wǒde zìxíngchē diū le, xiàwǔ qiánbāo yòu bèitōu le. It's luckless, I lost my bicycle in the morning and my wallet was stolen in the afternoon!
下午	xiàwǔ	afternoon	
中午	zhōngwǔ	noon	
午饭	wǔfàn	lunch	

小提示 Tips	“午”的第一笔是短撇，第二笔横与第一笔相接。 The first stroke of “午” is a short left-falling stroke that links with the top horizontal stroke.

					西 xī
	甲骨文 Oracle bone script	金文 Bronze inscriptions	小篆 Small seal script	汉简 Han Bamboo script	楷书 Regular script

"西"，甲骨文和金文中，象鸟巢之形，所以"西"的本义指"鸟归巢栖息"。后"西"用来表示方向，与"东"相对。
The earliest form of "西" is a pictograph of bird nest, therefore "西" originally means "birds fly back to their nest". Later "西" is used to indicate the west, the opposite of the east.

一 丆 丙 丙 两 西

东西	dōngxī	east and west	西北	xīběi	northwest
	dōngxi	thing	西瓜	xīguā	watermelon
西边	xībiān	west	西部	xībù	western part
			西餐	xīcān	Western-style food
			西南	xīnán	southwest
			西方	xīfāng	the west
			西面	xīmiàn	west side
			西红柿	xīhóngshì	tomato

小提示 Tips	在现代汉语中，"西"通常用来指方向"西边"。 In modern Chinese, "西" usually means west.

	甲骨文 Oracle bone script	金文 Bronze inscriptions	小篆 Small seal script	楷书 Regular script
				下 xià

“下”，甲骨文和金文字形相同，上面一长横表示地面，下面一短横是指事符号，表示地面之下。小篆字形加了一竖，楷书字形将一竖拉直，成为现代字形。

The concept of down and below is clarified in relation to a horizontal line. The stroke below the fundamental line was originally a short line, embellished and finally stabilized “下”.

一丅下

下边	xià · bian	below	底下	dǐ · xia	below
下课	xiàkè	finish class	地下	dìxià	underground
下来	xiàlái	come down	下班	xiàbān	come or go off work
下去	xiàqù	go down	下面	xiàmiàn	below
下午	xiàwǔ	afternoon	乡下	xiāngxià	countryside
一下	yīxià	one time/once	以下	yǐxià	below/the following
			之下	zhīxià	under
			一下子	yīxià · zi	at one blow

小提示 Tips	“下”在书写时，第三笔“丶”在竖笔的右边。 The dot of “下” is put on the right of the vertical stroke.

甲骨文	金文	小篆	向 xiàng
甲骨文 Oracle bone script	金文 Bronze inscriptions	小篆 Small seal script	楷书 Regular script

“向”，甲骨文和金文字形像一座房子在墙壁上开了一个窗户。所以，“向”的本义专指“朝北的窗户”。后来，引申为“方向”或“朝向”之义。

The earliest form of “向” is an ideograph of a house with a window. In ancient times, houses usual faced south while window faced north, so “向” originally meant “windows facing north”. By extension, it means “direction” or “orientation”.

方向 fāngxiàng direction	你的房间面向哪个方向？ Nǐde fángjiān miànxiàng nǎgè fāngxiàng? Which direction does your room face?

小提示 Tips	“向”的第一笔是短撇，要注意与“回”相区分。 The first stroke of “向” is a short left-falling stroke. Be aware of the difference between “向” and “回”.

	甲骨文 Oracle bone script	金文 Bronze inscriptions	小篆 Small seal script	小 xiǎo 楷书 Regular script

"小"，甲骨文和金文是用三个小点表示，小篆字形将中间一点拉长拉直，左右两点变为一撇一捺。楷书将中间一竖变为竖钩，成为现代字形。

The earliest form of "小" is made up of three dots, which are pictograph of sands or other tiny things. Later the middle dot is straightened to a line and finally stabilized to "小".

亅 小 小

小姐	xiǎojiě	Miss
小时	xiǎoshí	hour
小孩儿	xiǎoháir	child
大小	dàxiǎo	size
小麦	xiǎomài	wheat
小心	xiǎoxīn	be careful
小学	xiǎoxué	primary school
小说	xiǎoshuō	novel
小伙子	xiǎohuǒ · zi	chap
小朋友	xiǎopéngyǒu	children

小提示 Tips

"小"字先写中间的竖钩，再写左边的撇，最后写右边的点。

The writing of "小" begins with the vertical hook in the middle, then the left-falling stroke and finally the right dot.

	甲骨文 Oracle bone script	金文 Bronze inscriptions	小篆 Small seal script	楷书 Regular script
				心 xīn

"心"，甲骨文和金文中，象人的心脏之形，故本义指"心脏"。小篆中，笔画变得对称圆滑。到了楷书，笔画省减且拉直。

The earliest form of "心" is like people's heart, so it means heart originally. The form of "心" in small seal script tends to be symmetrical, and with straightening out it becomes the modern reinforced form "心".

丶 心 心 心

点心	diǎnxīn	pastry
关心	guānxīn	care/caring
担心	dānxīn	worry/worried
决心	juéxīn	to make up one's mind
耐心	nàixīn	patient /patiently
热心	rèxīn	warmhearted/heartily
伤心	shāngxīn	heartrending
细心	xìxīn	careful
小心	xiǎoxīn	be careful
心情	xīnqíng	mood

以心为意符的字 Characters with "心" to signify meaning	意符在下：感、忽、急、念、态、忘、息、思、想、意、愿、志
小提示 Tips	为了书写的方便，"心"作为偏旁在隶书中通常写作"忄"，如："怕"、"情"、"愉"；由"心"或"忄"组成的字，大多与心情或情绪有关。 In order to write more conveniently, "心" as a radical sometimes is written as "忄" in clerical script which has been retained today; the characters with "心" or "忄" mostly refer to emotion.

甲骨文 Oracle bone script	金文 Bronze inscriptions	小篆 Small seal script	楷书 Regular script
			辛 xīn

“辛”，甲骨文字形像一把平头刀的样子，上部是刀头，下部是刀把。金文字形的上部加了一横，小篆字形的下部又加了一横。“辛”的本义指“刀”，因为用刀劳动是件辛苦的事，所以“辛”引申有“辛苦”之义。

“辛” is a pictograph of a knife that the upper part is the cutting head and the lower part is the hilt. Later people added a horizontal over the cutting head. Originally “辛” means knife, as to work with a knife can be hard, “辛” extends to mean hard.

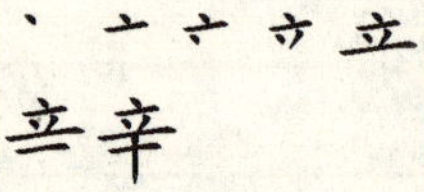

辛苦　xīnkǔ　hard

辛苦工作了四个小时后，他觉得非常饿。

Xīnkǔ gōngzuò le sìgè xiǎoshí hòu, tā juéde fēicháng è.

He felt very hungry after four-hours' hard work.

小提示 Tips

注意区别“辛”与“幸”。

It should be noted that “辛” and “幸” are different.

<table>
<tr><td rowspan="2"></td><td></td><td></td><td></td><td>行 xíng
háng</td></tr>
<tr><td>甲骨文
Oracle
bone script</td><td>金文
Bronze
inscriptions</td><td>小篆
Small
seal script</td><td>楷书
Regular script</td></tr>
<tr><td colspan="4">“行”，甲骨文和金文字形像十字路口，东西南北皆能通行。所以，“行”的本义指“路”。因为有路就可以行走，故“行”又引申为动词“行走”。
The earliest form of “行” is a pictograph of a crossroad that people could pass freely in all directions, therefore “行” originally means roads. By extension, it means “walk”.</td><td></td></tr>
</table>

进行	jìnxíng	be underway	不行	bùxíng	no way
旅行	lǚxíng	travel	举行	jǔxíng	hold
自行车	zìxíngchē	bicycle	实行	shíxíng	put into practice
银行	yínháng	bank	送行	sòngxíng	see somebody off
			行动	xíngdòng	action
			行李	xínglǐ	baggage
			执行	zhíxíng	execute

小提示 Tips

“行”有两种读音：当“行”作动词时，通常读为“xíng”，如：进行、旅行；当“行”作名词时，通常读为“háng”，如：银行、行列、行伍、行业。

“行” has two different readings. When used as a verb, it should be pronounced as “xíng”, for example, “进行” or “旅行”; when used as a noun, it usually reads “háng”, for example, “银行”，“行列”，“行伍” and “行业”.

	甲骨文 1 Oracle bone script 1	甲骨文 2 Oracle bone script 2	小篆 Small seal script	幸 xìng 楷书 Regular script

"幸"，甲骨文字形像一双桎梏、手铐，用以钳住犯人或奴隶的两个手腕，所以"幸"的本义指"手铐"。而不被手铐、桎梏所钳，则是幸运、幸福的事情，故"幸"引申有"幸福"之义。这是古文字中常见的"反义为训"现象。

The earliest form of "幸" is a pictograph of an ancient handcuffs, which is used to shackle prisoners' or slaves' hands, so "幸" originally means handcuffs. For people, not being shackled by handcuffs is lucky and happy, so "幸" is extended to mean happy.

一 十 土 土 圥 坴 坴 幸

幸福 xìngfú happy/happiness	不幸 bùxìng unfortunate/misfortune

小提示 Tips	注意区别"辛"与"幸"。 It should be noted that "辛" and "幸" are different.

				須	须 xū
	甲骨文 Oracle bone script	金文 Bronze inscriptions	小篆 Small seal script	楷书（繁体） Regular script (complex form)	楷书（简体） Regular script (simplified form)

"须"，甲骨文中像人侧面站立，突出了大大的嘴巴和几根胡须，所以"须"指的就是胡须。金文中，人的身体变小，突出了面部和面部的三根胡须。到了小篆，由于字形变化，三根胡须已与面部分离。

The earliest form of "须" was in the shape of a man standing sideways with his mouse and beard highlighted, so it meant beard originally. Its form changed in small seal script and regular script: the three sweep to the left, symbolizing beard, had separated with the right part which symbolized people's face and body.

必须 bìxū must/ to have to	必须得想个办法。 Bìxū děi xiǎng gè bànfǎ. Something must be done about it.
小提示 Tips	"须"的繁体字字形是"須"，本义指"胡须"，后来指"必须"或"应当"时是记音。 The original complex form of "须" is "須"; the original meaning of "须" is "beard", and later the character is used to mean "must" or "should".

	甲骨文 Oracle bone script	金文 Bronze inscriptions	小篆 Small seal script	言 yán 楷书 Regular script

"言"，甲骨文和金文中，像舌头从口中伸出，所以"言"表示"说话"、"讲话"之义。到了楷书，"言"下部的"口"没有改变，但上部的"舌头"拉直，变为三横。

The earliest form of "言" looks like tongue out of mouth, so it means speaking and talking originally. The written form in regular script is changed that the tongue is straightened to three lines with a dot above.

语言 yǔyán language	发言 fāyán speak/ statement

以言为意符的字 Characters with "言" to signify pronunciation	意符在右：信
小提示 Tips	"言"作为偏旁时，通常写作"讠"，如：词、调、读、话、讲、论、评、说、诉、谈、谢、语；由"言"或"讠"组成的字大多与说话有关。 "言" as a radical is usually written as "讠", such as "词", "调", "读", "话", "讲", "论", "评", "说", "诉", "谈", "谢" and "语"; the characters with "言" or "讠" mostly refer to talking or speaking.

			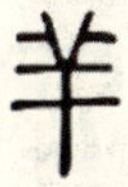	羊 yáng
	甲骨文 Oracle bone script	金文 Bronze inscriptions	小篆 Small seal script	楷书 Regular script

“羊”，甲骨文和金文中，上部就像是羊头顶向下弯曲的犄角，特别突出了犄角之形。在小篆中，两边向下的犄角被拉直，楷书字体与小篆接近。 The earliest form of “羊” is a pictograph of sheepshead. The upper part represents the sheep’s decurved horn, which is highlighted. Later the horn is straightened into new form “羊”.	丶 丷 䒑 ⺷ 兰 羊
羊 yáng sheep	我们的羊离开羊群走失了。 Wǒmen de yáng líkāi yángqún zǒushī le. Our sheep have strayed from the fold.
以羊为声符的字 Characters with “羊” to signify pronunciation	声符在右：样 yàng
小提示 Tips	“羊”作为偏旁时，通常写作“⺶”，如“羚”。 “羊” as a radical is usually written as “⺶”, such as “羚”.

				也 yě
	金文 Bronze inscriptions	小篆 Small seal script	隶书 Clerical script	楷书 Regular script

"也"，金文中，像蛇形。后借用来作语气词或助词，且通常放在句尾，表示判断或肯定。在现代汉语中，"也"通常用作副词，表示"同样"。

The earliest form of "也" is a pictograph of a snake. Later "也" is used as a modal particle or a particle, placed at the end of a sentence, to indicate affirmation. Now "也" is used as an adverb to indicate "also" or "as well as".

也许 yěxǔ perhaps/maybe	既……也……	jì…yě…	as well as
	一……也……	yī…yě…	as well

小提示 Tips

在上古时代，"也"与"它"、"虫"意思相同，都指蛇。

In ancient times, the three characters："也"，"它" and "虫" have the same meaning, all of which refer to snake.

	甲骨文 Oracle bone script	金文 Bronze inscriptions	小篆 Small seal script	楷书（繁体） Regular script （complex form）	楷书（简体） Regular script （simplified form）
				頁	页 yè

"页"，甲骨文中像人侧身跽坐，特别突出了人头，所以"页"本义指"头"。金文字形的下部已经不太像人体了，但上部的头仍然很清晰。小篆下部的人体，到楷书中变成撇与点，更不象形。

The form of "页" in oracle bone script is in the shape of a man sitting sideways with his head highlighted, so "页" means head originally. We still could find the head from "页" in bronze, while the body below isn't pictographic. And now it is simplified to "页".

一 丆 丆 丙 页 页

页码 yèmǎ page number	注意页码要写清楚。 Zhùyì yèmǎ yào xiě qīngchu. Take care that the pages are clearly numbered.
以页为意符的字 Characters with "页" to signify meaning	意符在右：顿 烦 顾 领 颜 意符在右上角：题
小提示 Tips	由"页"组成的字，大都与头有关，例如：顿、烦、顾、领、题、颜；现代汉语中，"页"经常用作量词，如：一页书。 The characters with "页" mostly refer to head, such as "顿", "烦", "顾", "领", "题" and "颜"; while in modern Chinese it is often used as a measure word, such as "一页书".

	一	一	一	一 yī
	甲骨文 Oracle bone script	金文 Bronze inscriptions	小篆 Small seal script	楷书 Regular script

"一"，从甲骨文、金文、小篆到楷书，字形都相同，画一横表示数字"一"。所以，"一"最初是记数的符号。后来引申有"专一"、"统一"等义项。

From ancient times to now, we always draw a horizontal to indicate "一". At first, "一" is just used to write down the number "one". Then it extends to mean single-minded or unified.

一

一般	yībān	commonly			
一定	yīdìng	surely	一半	yībàn	half
一共	yīgòng	in all	一边	yībiān	one side/at the same time
一起	yīqǐ	together	一齐	yīqí	in concert
一切	yīqiè	every	一生	yīshēng	all one's life
一下	yīxià	one time/all of a sudden	一时	yīshí	for a short while
一些	yīxiē	some	一同	yītóng	in the company of
一样	yīyàng	the same	一致	yīzhì	consistent
一直	yīzhí	always	一道	yīdào	together
一点儿	yīdiǎnr	a little	之一	zhīyī	one of (something)
一块儿	yīkuàir	together	统一	tǒngyī	unify/unification
一会儿	yīhuìr	for a moment			

小提示 Tips	"一"在书写时，从左往右写，要写平。 The character "一" goes straight forward from left to right.

<table>
<tr><td rowspan="2"> </td><td> </td><td> </td><td> </td><td>衣 yī</td></tr>
<tr><td>甲骨文
Oracle
bone script</td><td>金文
Bronze
inscriptions</td><td>小篆
Small
seal script</td><td>楷书
Regular script</td></tr>
<tr><td colspan="4">“衣”，甲骨文和金文中，象衣服之形，上部是衣领，两侧的开口处是袖口。所以“衣”的本义指“衣服”，现在这一义项仍然是最常用的。
The earliest form of “衣” is a pictograph of a coat that the upper part is collar and the each side is sleeve. So originally “衣” means clothes, and now we still use it to mean clothes.</td><td></td></tr>
</table>

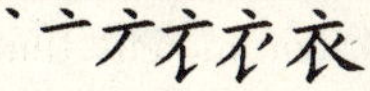

衣服 yīfu clothes			
	衬衣	chènyī	shirt
	大衣	dàyī	overcoat
	毛衣	máoyī	sweater
	棉衣	miányī	cotton-padded clothes
	上衣	shàngyī	coat/jacket
	雨衣	yǔyī	raincoat
	洗衣机	xǐyījī	washing machine

以衣为意符的字 Characters with “衣” to signify meaning	意符在下：装 意符在右：被　袜　初
小提示 Tips	为了书写的方便，“衣”作为偏旁在楷书中通常写作“衤”并沿用至今，如：被、袜、初。 In order to write more conveniently, “衣” as a radical sometimes is written as “衤” in regular script which has been retained today, for example, “被”, “袜” and “初”.

	ㄹ	已 yǐ
	小篆 Small seal script	楷书 Regular script
	小篆中的“已”和“己”本是同一个字（参见“己”）。现在，“已”不作任何字的部件，作声旁的都是“己”部件。“已”目前都用作“已经”、“而已”的“已”。 The characters “已” and “己” are two different writings while have the same meaning in small seal script（see“己”）. In modern Chinese，“己” could be a radical of other characters while “已” can't. “已” is usually used in the words such as “已经” and “而已”.	㇕ ㇕ 已

已经 yǐjīng already	我已经吃饱了。 Wǒ yǐjīng chībǎo le. I've had enough.

小提示 Tips	“已”的最后一笔要与第二笔横相接并出头，但与第一笔横折相离。 The final stroke of “已” is connected with horizontal stroke and exceeds it, but is separated from the first stroke horizontal turning.

金文 Bronze inscriptions	小篆 Small seal script	楷书 Regular script
		音 yīn

"音"，金文中，象舌头伸出嘴巴之形，与"言"造字结构相似，故"音"的本义指"人发出的声音"。现在，"音"可以指各种不同的声音。

The written form of "音" in bronze is like tongue out of mouth, so it originally means "sound or voice of people". Now "音" is used to indicate different sounds made by people, animal or musical instruments.

录音	lùyīn	recording	语音	yǔyīn	voice
声音	shēngyīn	sound/voice	录音机	lùyīnjī	recorder
音乐	yīnyuè	music	收音机	shōuyīnjī	radio

以音为意符的字 Characters with "音" to signify meaning	意符在上：章
小提示 Tips	在古汉语中，"声"指乐器发出的响声，"音"指人发出的声音；在现代汉语中，两个字合在一起，"声音"指一切响声。 In ancient Chinese, "声" referred to sound of musical instrument, while "音" indicated voice of people. In modern Chinese, "声" and "音" are put together to mean all sound.

			永 yǒng
甲骨文 Oracle bone script	金文 Bronze inscriptions	小篆 Small seal script	楷书 Regular script

"永"，甲骨文、金文和小篆中，像一人侧身在水中游泳，所以"永"本义指"游泳"，后用来形容水势长流的样子，进而引申为"久远"、"深远"之义。

The ancient form of "永" is like a man swimming in a river, even we could see the flowing water. It means swimming originally, and then is used to represent flowing water, from which comes the ideograph "everlasting".

永远 yǒngyuǎn forever/eternal	我们将永远怀念他。 Wǒmen jiāng yǒngyuǎn huáiniàn tā. We will embalm him forever.
以永为声符的字 Characters with "永" to signify pronunciation	声符在右：泳 yǒng
小提示 Tips	"永"的第二画"横折钩"是一笔写成，不能分成两笔。 The second stroke of "永" should be written without being broken.

甲骨文 Oracle bone script	金文 Bronze inscriptions	小篆 Small seal script	用 yòng 楷书 Regular script

"用"，甲骨文、金文和小篆字形十分接近，象木桶之形。因古代祭祀时，把杀好的牲畜装在桶里，而引申为"施用"之义。

The ancient form of "用" is in the shape of a wooden cask. As in ancient times, people generally put killed livestock in cask in sacrifice, "用" is extended to mean "use".

丿 冂 月 月 用

不用	bùyòng	need not
利用	lìyòng	make use of
使用	shǐyòng	use
采用	cǎiyòng	adopt
没用	méiyòng	it is no use
费用	fèiyòng	expense
耐用	nàiyòng	durable
实用	shíyòng	practicable
适用	shìyòng	suitable for use
应用	yìngyòng	apply
用处	yòngchù	usefulness
用功	yònggōng	hardworking
有用	yǒuyòng	useful
运用	yùnyòng	to use
作用	zuòyòng	effect

小提示
Tips

"用"字先写外面再写里面，最后一竖与两横相交。

The outer strokes of "用" is written before inner ones, and its final vertical stroke goes across two horizontal strokes.

<table>
<tr><td rowspan="2"></td><td></td><td></td><td></td><td></td><td>尤 yóu</td></tr>
<tr><td>甲骨文
Oracle
bone script</td><td>金文
Bronze
inscriptions</td><td>小篆
Small
seal script</td><td>隶书
Clerical script</td><td>楷书
Regular script</td></tr>
<tr><td colspan="5">“尤”，甲骨文和金文中，象手臂之形，上有一斜画指手臂上长了某种东西，所以“尤”的本义指“肉瘤”。古人认为长在手臂上的瘤是不正常的，由此引申出“特别”、“特异”之义。
The form of “尤” in oracle bone and bronze is like an arm. There is a tumor on the upper limb, so man adds a stroke to highlight. Therefore, “尤” originally means “tumor on arms”. As ancients thought tumor was monstrous, it extended to mean “ special” or “unusual”.</td><td>一 ナ 九 尤</td></tr>
<tr><td colspan="3">尤其 yóuqí especially/ particularly</td><td colspan="3">我喜欢乡村，尤其是春天的乡村。
Wǒ xǐhuān xiāngcūn, yóuqí shì chūntiān de xiāngcūn.
I love country, especially in spring.</td></tr>
<tr><td colspan="2">以尤为意符的字
Characters with “尤” to signify meaning</td><td colspan="4">意符在右：就</td></tr>
<tr><td colspan="2">小提示
Tips</td><td colspan="4">在上古时代，“尤”的本义是“肉瘤”。但在现代汉语中，“尤”通常用作副词，表示“尤其”、“特别”之义。
In ancient times, “尤” referred to tumor on arms. While in modern Chinese, “尤” is mostly used as an adverb to express “ especially” or “particularly”.</td></tr>
</table>

	甲骨文 Oracle bone script	金文 Bronze inscriptions	小篆 Small seal script	又 yòu 楷书 Regular script

"又"，甲骨文、金文和小篆中，象右手之形，只是将手的五指减为三指。所以"又"本义指"人的右手"，后用作副词是记音，表"再"、"再次"之义。

The ancient form of "又" looks like people's right hand. As Chinese in ancient time generally used three to represent "a lot", five fingers were simplified to three ones. It originally means right hand, later is used as an adverb to express "again".

ㄱ 又

既……又…… jì...yòu... not only...but also	这个餐厅的食物既便宜又好吃。 Zhègè cāntīng de shíwù jì piányi yòu hǎochī. This restaurant's foods are cheap and tasty.
以又为意符的字 Characters with "又" to signify meaning	意符在右下角：般　报　服　设　友 意符在下：变　度 意符在右：取
小提示 Tips	由"又"组成的字，大多与"手"有关。 The characters with "又", mostly refer to actions you have to use your hands.

				魚	鱼 yú
	甲骨文 Oracle bone script	金文 Bronze inscriptions	小篆 Small seal script	楷书（繁体） Regular script (complex form)	楷书（简体） Regular script (simplified form)

"鱼"，甲骨文和金文中，字形像一条鱼，身上有鳞，两侧有鳍。在小篆中，字形有了较大变化，特别是代表鱼鳍的两撇，移到了尾部。而楷书中，鱼尾则变为一横，更不象形了。

The earliest form of "鱼" is a pictograph of a fish, even we could see its scales, fins and tail. Later the form of "鱼" has been changed: the two strokes, stands for fins, are removed to its tail. Now its tail changes into a horizontal, and isn't like a fish any more.

金鱼	jīnyú	goldfish	渔大收了网，发现有一条人金鱼在里面。 Yúfū shōu le wǎng, fāxiàn yǒu yītiáo dà jīnyú zài lǐmiàn. The fisher drew in the net and found a big goldfish in it.
鲸鱼	jīngyú	whale	

小提示 Tips	由"鱼"组成的字，通常与鱼有关。 Characters with "鱼" as radical mostly refer to a kind of fish.

甲骨文 Oracle bone script	金文 Bronze inscriptions	小篆 Small seal script	楷书 Regular script
			雨 yǔ

"雨"，甲骨文和金文中，像雨点从天空落下的样子。
The earliest form of "雨" is an ideograph that the upper line stands for the sky, and the dots represent the drip-drops, which means it is raining.

雨衣 yǔyī raincoat	没带雨衣那就先避一下雨。 Méidài yǔyī nàjiù xiān bìyīxià yǔ. Do keep out of the rain if you haven't a coat.
以雨为意符的字 Characters with "雨" to signify meaning	意符在上：零 雪 需
小提示 Tips	"雨"作为偏旁，常常放在字的上部，如上面提到的零、雪、需；由"雨"组成的字，大多与云、雨有关，如：雪、霜。 As a radical, "雨" is usually written in the top of a character, such as the characters mentioned above; the characters with "雨" mostly refer to cloud or rain.

	ㄎ	𠀀	𠀁	元 yuán
	甲骨文 Oracle bone script	金文 Bronze inscriptions	小篆 Small seal script	楷书 Regular script

“元”，甲骨文和金文中，下部像人侧面站立，上部的“二”指人的头部，故“元”的本义指“人头”。到了小篆和楷书，上部表示头部的“二”没有变化，下部表示人身体的笔画发生了改变。 The earliest form of “元” is in the shape of a man standing sideways with two lines “二” above, which represent the man’s head, so “元” means people’s head originally. Later the down part finally stabilized “元”.	一 二 亍 元

公元	gōngyuán	Christian era/A. D.
美元	měiyuán	U. S. dollar
日元	rìyuán	Japanese yen

以元为声符的字 Characters with “元” to signify pronunciation	声符在内：园 yuán 声符在右：院 yuàn 声符在右上角：远 yuǎn
小提示 Tips	“元”的本义指“人的头”，因为“头”是人身体最上端的部分，所以一个国家最重要的人（最高领导者）称为“元首”。 The original meaning of “元” is people’s head. As head is thought to be the top part of one’s body, the most important person of a country (president) is called “元首”.

	𝔇	𝔇	𝔇	月 yuè
	甲骨文 Oracle bone script	金文 Bronze inscriptions	小篆 Small seal script	楷书 Regular script

"月"即月亮，甲骨文象弯月之形。金文在中间加一点，是为了与"夕"区别。经过小篆的变化，就成了楷书的"月"。 The character "月" represents the moon, oracle bone script is the shape of crescent . In order to distinguish from the character "夕" (sunset), people add a dot in the middle of bronze inscription character. After the evolution of small seal script, it turns into regular script character.	丿 月 月 月

月	yuè	the moon
月亮	yuè · liang	the moon
月球	yuèqiú	the moon

以月为意符的字 Characters with "月" to signify meaning	意符在右：明　期　朝　阴 意符在右上角：望
小提示 Tips	"明"、"望"、"朝"、"期"等：其中的"月"（yuè）是月亮变来的。 "月" in characters such as "明", "望", "朝" and "期" is transformed from character "月" (the moon). "湖"、"脚"、"脸"、"脏"等：其中的"月"是"肉"（ròu）变来的。参见"肉"字。 "月" in characters such as "湖", "脚", "脸" and "脏" is transformed from character "肉" (meat). "服"、"胜"等：其中的"月"是"舟"（zhōu）变来的。参见"服"字。 "月" in characters such as "服" and "胜" is transformed from character "舟" (boat).

	甲骨文 Oracle bone script	金文 Bronze inscriptions	小篆 Small seal script	楷书（繁体） Regular script (complex form)	楷书（简体） Regular script (simplified form)
				樂	乐 yuè lè

"乐"，甲骨文字形像琴弦系在木上。金文字形中，加了调弦的工具。所以"乐"的本义指"乐器"，后引申为"音乐"。音乐能使人快乐，"乐"再引申有"快乐"、"安乐"等意义。

The ancient form of "乐" is a pictograph of an ancient musical instrument. Later people add a tuning page to it. So "乐" originally means a musical instrument, then extends to mean music. As music could bring happiness to people, by extension, it means "happy" or "peaceful".

一 匚 乒 乐 乐

音乐 yīnyuè music	我喜欢古典音乐，不太喜欢流行音乐。 Wǒ xǐhuān gǔdiǎn yīnyuè, bù tài xǐhuān liúxíng yīnyuè. I prefer classical music to pop music.

小提示 Tips	"乐"有两种读音："乐"作名词指音乐、乐器时，读为"yuè"；"乐"作形容词指快乐、欢乐时，读为"lè"。 "乐" has two different readings. When indicating "music" or "musical instrument", it should be pronounced as "yuè", and when indicating "happy" or "joyful", it should be read "lè".

				云 yún
	甲骨文 1 Oracle bone script 1	甲骨文 2 Oracle bone script 2	小篆 Small seal script	楷书 Regular script

“云”，甲骨、金文和小篆字形，均像天空中云气回旋飘拂的样子，上部的两横表示云层，下部的曲线表示卷状的云团。

“云” is a pictograph of floating clouds. When the humid and warm vapours rise and reach the colder regions, they condense and form clouds. The upper two lines stand for the clouds, and the lower curve represents the floating vapours.

一 二 云 云

乌云　wūyún　black clouds 云彩　yúncǎi　cloud	乌云密布预示着将要下雨。 Wūyún mìbù yùshì zhe jiāngyào xiàyǔ. The black clouds threatened rain. 云彩把月亮遮得看不清楚。 Yúncǎi bǎ yuèliang zhēde kànbù qīngchǔ. Clouds blotting out the moon.
以云为声符的字 Characters with “云” to signify pronunciation	声符在右上角：运　yùn
小提示 Tips	“云”的繁体字字形是“雲”。 The original complex form of “云” was “雲”.

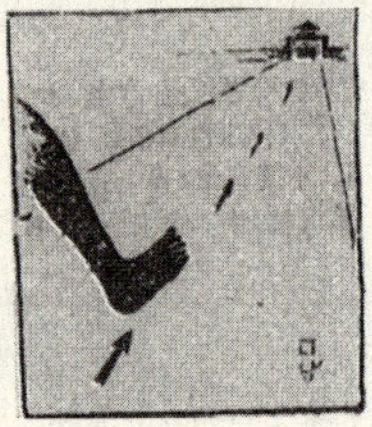

	甲骨文 Oracle bone script	金文 Bronze inscriptions	小篆 Small seal script	正 zhèng 楷书 Regular script

"正"，甲骨文中，上面的部件表示方国城邑，下面的部件指人脚，上下合起来表示向方国城邑进伐，所以"正"本义是"征伐"，后来引申为"中正"、"不偏斜"之义。 The written form of "正" in oracle bone is made up of two parts: the upper part represents cities and towns, and the down part represents people's foot. The two parts are put together literally to mean "go on a punitive expedition", later extend to mean "fair" or "just".	一 丅 下 𤴓 正

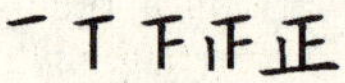

真正	zhēnzhèng	true/real/ genuine
正确	zhèngquè	correct
正在	zhèngzài	in the process of
反正	fǎnzhèng	anyway
改正	gǎizhèng	to correct
纠正	jiūzhèng	to make right
正常	zhèngcháng	ordinary/normal/regular
正好	zhènghǎo	just right
正式	zhèngshì	formal

以正为意符的字 Characters with "正" to signify meaning	意符在下：整 意符在左：政
以正为声符的字 Characters with "正" to signify pronunciation	声符在下：整 zhěng 声符在左：政 zhèng

	支	支	支	支 zhī
	小篆 Small seal script	汉简 Han bamboo script	隶书 Clerical script	楷书 Regular script

"支"，金文和小篆中，像用手抓住树枝、竹枝之类的东西，故"支"的本义是"树枝"、"竹枝"等，后来用来指"分支"的"支"。

The ancient form of "支" is like a hand grabbing branches or bamboo branches, so it originally means "branches". Later it is used to express "embranchment", and another character "枝" is produced to represent "branches".

一 十 [illegible] 支

支持	zhīchí	support	我完全支持你。 Wǒ wánquán zhīchí nǐ. I'll support you to the hilt.
支援	zhīyuán	provide assistance or backing	

小提示 Tips

在古汉语中，"支"的本义是"树枝"，因为树枝常用来支撑物体，所以在现代汉语中，"支"有"支撑"之义，如"支持"、"支援"等。

In ancient Chinese, the original meaning of "支" was branches. As people usually use branches to support objects, "支" means support in modern Chinese.

	甲骨文 Oracle bone script	金文 Bronze inscriptions	小篆 Small seal script	之 zhī 楷书 Regular script
"之"，甲骨文中，上部指人脚，下部是表示地面的一横，两部分合起来表示人从某处出发，所以"之"的本义是"往"、"到某处去"。 The form of "之" in oracle bone has two components: upper component represents people's foot, and the line represents horizon. The two components are put together literally to mean "to set off" or "go to some place".				丶 ㇇ 之

……分之……	...fēnzhī... indicating a fraction	之前	zhīqián	in front of/ before
		之后	zhīhòu	behind/after
……之间……	...zhījiān... between/among	之上	zhīshàng	above
		之下	zhīxià	below
		之一	zhīyī	one of (something)
		之中	zhīzhōng	inside

小提示 Tips	在古代汉语中，"之"作动词或代词，有实际意义；在现代汉语中，"之"通常作助词，只有语法作用，没有实际意义。 In ancient Chinese, "之" had substantive meanings and was mostly used as a verb or pronoun. In modern Chinese, "之" is usually used as a particle and just has grammar effect.

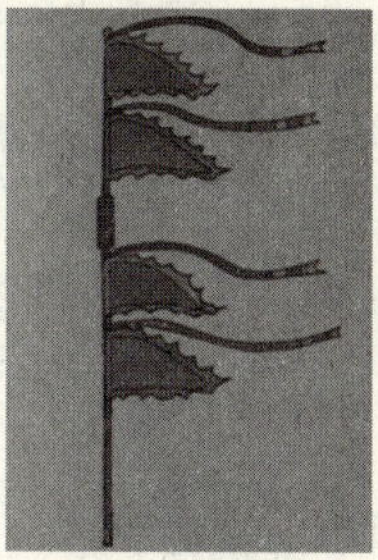				中 zhōng zhòng
	甲骨文 Oracle bone script	金文 Bronze inscriptions	小篆 Small seal script	楷书 Regular script

"中"，甲骨文和金文字形像一面旗帜。一竖是旗杆，向右弯曲的四条线是飘带，"口"形就是指明"旗杆的中间"，所以"中"的本义指"中间"。到了小篆和楷书，字形简化为"中"。

"中" is a pictograph of a flag. The "丨" stands for flagpole, and the four curved lines represent streamers. The "口" in the middle of flagpole indicates where the center is. Later in order to write easily, people omitted the four curved lines and produced the regular form "中".

丨 冂 口 中

中间	zhōngjiān	middle
中午	zhōngwǔ	noon
中学	zhōngxué	high school
中文	zhōngwén	Chinese

集中	jízhōng	centralize
空中	kōngzhōng	in the air
其中	qízhōng	among/in (which)
之中	zhīzhōng	in
中心	zhōngxīn	center
中央	zhōngyāng	centre/central authorities
中餐	zhōngcān	Chinese food/lunch
中药	zhōngyào	traditional Chinese medicine

以中为声符的字
Characters with "中" to signify pronunciation

声符在右：钟 zhōng
种 zhǒng/zhòng

	甲骨文 1 Oracle bone script 1	甲骨文 2 Oracle bone script 2	小篆 Small seal script	主 zhǔ 楷书 Regular script
“主”，甲骨文字形由两部分组成，下部是木，上部像燃烧的火，中间一点即指火的中心。所以，“主”的本义指“灯芯”，后来指“主人”、“君主”等意义是记音。 The earliest form of “主” is an ideograph, which is combined with “木”（wood）and “火”（fire）, and the dot in fire stands for the fire corn. So originally “主” means lampwick, and then it is used to mean “master” or “emperor”.				丶 亠 二 丰 主

主要 zhǔyào main/mostly 主意 zhǔyì idea	民主 mínzhǔ democracy 主动 zhǔdòng initiative/active 主观 zhǔguān subjective 主人 zhǔrén master/host 主任 zhǔrèn director 主席 zhǔxí chairman 主张 zhǔzhāng proposal
以主为声符的字 Characters with “主” to signify pronunciation	声符在右：住 zhù 注 zhù
小提示 Tips	“王”字上面加一点就是“主”。 “主” can be composed by adding a dot to the top of “王”.

	(bronze script form)	(drum-stone form)	(clerical form)	子 zǐ
	金文 Bronze script	石鼓文 Inscriptions on drum-shaped stone	隶书 Clerical script	楷书 Regular script

"子"，金文像在襁褓中的小孩子。石鼓文与隶书将圆头写成三角了。楷书中，三角形的头又变成"乛"。

The bronze script "子" likes a baby in swaddling clothes. The baby's round head is converted into triangular in script on drum-shaped stone and clerical script. In regular script, the triangular head is turned into "乛".

乛 了 子

杯子	bēi · zi	cup	筷子	kuài · zi	chopsticks
孩子	hái · zi	children	盘子	pán · zi	plate
饺子	jiǎo · zi	dumpling	妻子	qī · zi	wife
样子	yàng · zi	appearance	裙子	qún · zi	skirt
桌子	zhuō · zi	desk	狮子	shī · zi	lion
鼻子	bí · zi	nose	兔子	tù · zi	rabbit
刀子	dāo · zi	knife	叶子	yè · zi	leaf
肚子	dù · zi	belly	看样子	kànyàng · zi	it looks as if
房子	fáng · zi	house	一下子	yīxià · zi	all at once
裤子	kù · zi	trousers	小伙子	xiǎohuǒ · zi	youngster

以子为意符的字 Characters with "子" to signify meaning	意符在下：学　字 意符在左：孩
以子为声符的字 Characters with "子" to signify pronunciation	声符在下：字 zì

甲骨文 Oracle bone script	金文 Bronze inscriptions	小篆 Small seal script	楷书 Regular script
			自 zì

"自"，甲骨文中，象鼻子之形，故本义指"鼻子"，可能古人在自称时常指着鼻子，后来用作第一人称代词"自己"之"自"。

The form of "自" in oracle bone is like people's nose, so "自" originally means nose. It was probably that the ancients tended to point at their noses when calling themselves, therefore "自" are used as the first person pronoun "I" or "me".

自己	zìjǐ	self
自行车	zìxíngchē	bicycle/bike
来自	láizì	to come from (a place)
亲自	qīnzì	personally
自从	zìcóng	since
自动	zìdòng	automatic
自费	zìfèi	at one's own expense
自觉	zìjué	conscious
自然	zìrán	nature
自我	zìwǒ	self
自学	zìxué	study on one's own
自由	zìyóu	freedom/free

以自为意符的字 Characters with "自" to signify meaning	意符在上：息
小提示 Tips	由"自"组成的汉字大多与"鼻子"或鼻子的功能有关，如：息、嗅。 The characters with "自" are often associated with nose or nose's function, for example, "息" and "嗅".

				走 zǒu
	甲骨文 Oracle bone script	金文 Bronze inscriptions	小篆 Small seal script	楷书 Regular script

"走"，甲骨文象一人摆动双臂，急速行走之形；金文中，下面加上了代表脚的"止"字，由字形可以看出"走"的本义是"急速行走"，也就是"跑"。现在通常指"步行"。

The form of "走" in oracle bone is like a man walking quickly with two arms flailing wildly. Later the component representing foot is added on. Even from the written form, we can see it originally means "walk quickly" or "run". Now we often use "走" to express "walk" not "run".

一十土丰丰赱走

走道 zǒudào aisle way/aisle	我喜欢靠走道的座位。 Wǒ xǐhuān kào zǒudào de zuòwèi. I prefer an aisle seat.
以走为意符的字 Characters with "走" to signify meaning	意符在左：起
小提示 Tips	"走"作为偏旁，在字的左侧时，捺笔拉长；由"走"组成的字，一般与疾走、跑动有关。 When used on the left of a character, "走" is written with a longer right falling. The characters with "走" are mostly associated with fast walking or running.

	甲骨文 Oracle bone script	金文 Bronze inscriptions	小篆 Small seal script	楷书 Regular script
				足 zú

"足"，甲骨文中，象人的脚掌和股胫之形，故"足"指人的下肢。金文和小篆中，上部的股胫用圆圈表示，下部的脚掌也渐不象形。

The form of "足" in oracle bone is a picture of lower limbs with calf and foot , so "足" originally means people's lower limbs. Later man used a circle to represent calf, and derived the modern reinforced form "足".

足球 zúqiú football	充足 chōngzú sufficient/ abundant 满足 mǎnzú to satisfy
以足为意符的字 Characters with "足" to signify meaning	意符在左：践 路 跑 踢 跳 跟
小提示 Tips	为了书写的方便，"足"作为偏旁在隶书中通常写作"⻊"，如：跑、踢、跳；这些由"⻊"组成的字，通常与"脚"的动作有关。 In order to write more conveniently, "足" as a radical is usually written as "⻊" in clerical script, which has been retained today, such as the characters "跑", "踢" and "跳"; and most of them refer to actions done by foot.

附录：编写说明

绪 论

第一节 选题来源

对外汉字教学一直是对外汉语教学中的重点和难点。留学生的汉字认读和书写能力，直接影响到其对汉语的掌握。在现阶段的对外汉字教学中，汉字教学大多采用“随文识字”的方式，与词汇、阅读同时进行，而忽视汉字本身的规律性。这样势必会影响学生学习汉字的效果。因此，在针对留学生的汉字教学中，我们也需要对汉字本体进行研究，从汉字的规律性出发，与词汇、阅读教学相结合。那么，编写这样一本教材就非常有必要。

编写《学汉字 So Easy：中英双语图说汉字》出于以下两个方面的考虑：①以科学的理论研究为依据，设计一套针对非汉字文化圈初学者的汉字教学模板，解决对外汉字教学实践中的教材问题。本书希望设计出一套识字卡，以供教学者及自学者参考。②根据文献资料，可以了解到在20世纪90年代前期，汉字教学是附属于汉语教学的，相应的汉字教学教材少且不精。到了90年代后期，对外汉字教学的研究越来越受到重视，出现了较多对外汉字教材。从前人的研究成果中，笔者得到了大量有益的启示，但同时也发现，目前还没有一本将古文字知识、现代汉语知识以及英语结合起来的汉字教材。

第二节 研究的目的和意义

1990年至1991年，国家对外汉语教学领导办公室和北京语言大学联合研制了《汉语水平词汇与汉字等级大纲》，其中的“等级汉字”涵盖了留学生学习及考试用到的绝大部分汉字，是对外汉语汉字教学的主要依据。并且他们以字频、所对应的词汇分级为基础，将 2 905 个汉字分为甲、乙、丙、丁四级。

本书以《汉语水平词汇与汉字等级大纲》中的 800 个甲级字为研究材料，从中筛选出 148 个独体字，为每个独体字设计一张卡片，卡片力图把古文字知识与现代汉语教学结合起来，并配上英文翻译，以方便非汉字文化圈初学者学习。

目前的汉字教材大概可以分为三类：第一类是列出古文字字形，抓住汉字表意的特点，将字形与字义结合进行教学并配有英语翻译，但古文字字形解释简单粗糙甚至出现错误，如陈火平的《趣味汉字》；第二类是单纯列出汉字，将汉字与词汇、文章结合进行教学，但缺乏对字形、字义的讲解，如周健的《汉字突破》；第三类教材侧重于讲解古文字字形，列出古文字字形及其演变轨迹，讲解汉字字源，但所选汉字缺乏一定的标准和英文解释，不适合外国初学者，如熊国英的《图释古汉字》、佟大汶的《图解汉字》。

本书拟结合三类教材的优点，取长补短。这样不仅能填补目前对外汉字教材中的一项空白，也能在一定程度上提高对外汉字教学的效果。同时，汉字特别是古文字承载了中国传统文化，因此本书还有利于传播中国文化。

第三节　学术和应用价值

一、学术价值

本书的学术价值主要体现在以下三方面：①在研究课题的选择上具有一定的专业性。以如何设计科学的对外汉字教材为研究对象，从古文字学的角度切入，分析汉字的内部规律，如独体字字频高、笔画数少、难度系数低、具有能产性（能组合构成大量的合体字，是认识合体字的桥梁）、具有很强的理据性（象形简单直观，字形与字义结合紧密），结合现代汉语教学方法，试图在一定程度上解决汉字难学、难教的问题。②在研究方法上具有一定的科学性。在文献综述部分，使用文献分析法，得出目前对外汉字教材的特点和不足，在此基础上形成编写一本集各类汉字教材优点于一身的新教材的构思；在分析汉字内部规律的部分，使用观察统计法，首先对 800 个甲级字进行筛选，找出其中的 148 个独体字，然后在笔画数、难度系数以及能产性方面，对 148 个独体字进行数据分析，得出了独体字优先教学具有科学依据的结论；在字形教学部分，使用直观图画法，将字形与图片联系起来，加强了汉字学习的趣味性和直观性；在词汇教学部分，使用中英对照法，使得非汉字文化圈的初级学习者能够看懂；在词义教学部分，使用归纳演绎法，依据字形演绎字义。③在研究内容上具有一定的创新性。本书设计的识字卡结合了三类对外汉字教材的特点，在前人研究成果的基础上，取长补短，综合创新。首先是选择了800个甲级字中的148个独体字作为编写对象；其次列出古文字字形，展示汉字的演变过程，同时配合图片，增强了趣味性和直观性；再次，为该独体字配上甲级、乙级词汇，使得学习者在学习汉字的同时掌握其交际功能；最后，列出某字表示意义或读音的一系列字，以增强学习者对汉字结构特点的认识，扩展学习内容。同时本书还给整张识字卡配上了英文翻译，以方便非汉字文化圈初学者学习。

二、应用价值

本书的应用价值主要有以下四点：①设计一套方便、理想的对外汉字教材，为非汉字文化圈初学者提供一种汉字教学模板。目前的汉字教材内容丰富、形式各样。针对的学习群体、选择汉字的标准、汉字教材的内容以及编排的方法等，各有所长，不尽相同。这项研究以已有的科学理论研究为依据，从所针对的人群、汉字的选择到内容编排等方面，力求建立起一套较为合理的标准和较为科学的模板。②识字卡具有资料性和趣味性，能在一定程度上引发学习兴趣、提高学习效率，在对外汉字教学实践中有一定的使用价值。③无论学习者的知识水平是较低，还是略有基础，都可以选用这本书。此外，独体字的学习，可以按照人体、动物、植物、自然、人造物、数字等几个方面抽取排列，还可以按照构字能力强弱安排学习次序，加以抽取排列，有的字又可以按照文字学意义上的异同加以重新抽取排列。无论是“先语后文”，还是“语文同步”，甚至“文字独步”，对任何方法、任何教材，本书都方便配合，便于课堂教学与自学。④有利于传播中国传统文化，扩大其影响。汉字特别是古文字，是中国文化的重要载体。本书不仅提供了现代汉字资料，还列出了古文字字形、讲解了字源，让学习者在学习汉字的同时，也能深入了解中国传统文化。

第四节　国内外研究现状

一、国外研究现状

早在16世纪，西方传教士进入中国后，由于自身迫切需要学习汉语，同时也为了让更多的传教士学会汉语以便于传教，他们编写了不少汉语学习教材，如利玛窦的《葡华字典》、《西字奇迹》等。但这些教材主要是作为工具书使用的词典或字典，当时基本没有专门的汉字教材。

在20世纪初期，瑞典汉学家高本汉出于对汉语本身的兴趣，来到中国进行实地考察和研究。他在中国历代学者研究成果的基础上，运用欧洲比较语言学的方法，着重于汉语语音和汉字的演变，撰写了上百部相关著作，覆盖了汉语音韵学、方言学、词典学、文献学、考古学、文学、艺术和宗教等多个领域，在瑞典建立起专门的汉学学科。

其中，关于汉字的著作有《中日汉字分析字典》（*Analytical Dictionary of Chinese and Sino-Japanese*）和《古汉语字典》（*Grammata Serica*）。《中日汉字分析字典》于1923年在法国出版，由上古音、中古音、现代北京话发音、汉字字形字音和字义的说明构成。《古汉语字典》于1940年出版，将具有同一谐声成分的汉字都排在一起。对于所收汉字的字形，从甲骨文到铭文、碑文，再到现代字体，高本汉均按年代顺序作了标注；对于所收汉字的词源意义，凡是他认为确凿无疑的，也都一一作了标注；对于所收汉字的字音，每个字都标出了三个阶段的读音：他所构拟的汉语上古音、中古音和现代官话的读音。

20世纪80年代，在西方汉学研究领域，又出现了瑞典汉学家林西莉、法国汉学家白乐桑等人。林西莉是高本汉的学生，曾在50年代跟随他学习汉语。1989年，林西莉出版了专门研究汉字的《汉字王国》一书，里面收录了我们日常使用的汉字，她从字形上追根溯源，结合社会、经济、文化的变迁来讲述汉字的发展变化。

与高本汉、林西莉等人侧重汉语、汉字本体研究不同，白乐桑更侧重汉语、汉字的教学研究。他先后主编《汉语语法使用说明》、《汉字的表意王国》、《说字解词词典》等专著十余部，还与中国学者合作编写了《汉语语言文字启蒙》，该书在1989年出版后，成为法国各大学校最受欢迎的教材。

进入21世纪，由于国际交流更加频繁，汉语研究领域也吸引了更多的西方学者，汉字研究也渐渐独立出来，形成一个新的分支。2005年，德国美因兹大学教授顾安达专门组织了一场“汉字认知——西方学习者汉字认知研讨会”，研讨会吸引了中国、美国、法国、德国、英国、丹麦的40多位研究者聚集德国，共同探讨在对外汉语教学领域中的汉字学习问题，并在会后出版了《汉字的认知与教学——西方学习者汉字认知国际研讨会论文集》一书。

二、国内研究现状

1950年末，清华大学举办了“东欧交换生中国语文专修班”，由此中国开始了对外汉语教学实践，但当时还没有“对外汉语教学”这一名称，更没有形成一个专门学科。直到1982年4月，由北京语言学院（现北京语言大学）倡导，10所高校举行了一次会议，会议讨论建立一个研究对外国留学生进行汉语教学的学术团体，也就是在这次会议上，才确定了“对外汉语教学”这个名称，并在1983年成立了“对外汉语教学研究会”。而“对外汉字教学”则是在20世纪90年代中期以后才提出的，在此之前，汉字教学一直附属于汉语教学，没有独立地位。

以1996年召开的第五届国际汉语教学讨论会为分界点，对外汉字教学可分为前、后两期。

前期在教材方面的特点体现为：大部分基础汉语教材都有单独成册的汉字部分，如《基础汉语课本·汉字练习本》，但总体来说这一时期的基础汉语教材里汉字教学的内容并不突出；在中高级阶段，除了少量辨字组词之类的练习，则基本没有汉字教学内容；进入90年代，出现了一些专门以中高级留学生为对象的通论性汉字教材，如张静贤的《现代汉字教程》、李大遂的《简明实用汉字学》。

前期在对外汉字研究方面的特点体现为：1992年，国家汉办发表了《汉语水平词汇与汉字等级大纲》；吕必松的《对外汉语教学概论》、盛炎的《语言教学原理》、赵贤州的《对外汉语教学通论》等著作都涉及汉字和汉字教学的内容，但篇幅较短；这一时期还有一些研究汉字和汉字教学的论文，但研究者的注意力主要集中在教学方法和技巧层面，对汉字本体的关注较少。

后期在教材方面的特点体现为：出现了一大批针对初级留学生的汉字教材，内容丰富、形式多样。有将古文字知识与现代汉语结合起来的，如张惠芬的《张老师教汉字·汉字识写课本》、施正宇的《汉字津梁》、韩鉴堂的《汉字文化图说》，但韩书无英文翻译对照，对初学者来说有难度；有将汉字教学与词汇、文章相结合的，如周健的《汉字突破》，易洪川的《阶梯汉语·初级汉字》，孟慧颖、张英华的《HSK 汉字突破·2 000 个基本汉字精解》。

后期在对外汉字研究方面的特点体现为：1997 年 6 月，国家汉办在宜昌召开了首次汉字和汉字教学研讨会。1998 年 2 月，世界汉语教学学会和法国汉语教师协会联合在巴黎举办了国际汉字教学研讨会，会后出版了《汉字与汉字教学研究论文选》。此后，汉字教学方面的研究出现了高潮。对汉字本体的研究越来越多，深入到汉字笔画、笔顺、部件、构字法等方面；对形声字的研究，尤其是对声旁表音、形旁表义的功能研究，引起了对外汉语教学研究者的广泛关注；对汉字偏误、对外汉字教学规律的研究也出现了热点。很多研究，如万业馨、石定果、易洪川、施正宇、李大遂等学者的文章，都是建立在实验的基础之上，有数据、有统计、有分析，因而有说服力。此外，还出现了大量系统研究汉字的著作，如万业馨的《应用汉字学纲要》、孙德金的《对外汉字教学研究》、李香平的《汉字教学中的文字学》、周健的《汉字教学理论与方法》。还有将汉字教学与心理学、认知科学结合的著作，如江新的《对外汉语教学的心理学探索》，运用认知心理学的方法，对汉语包括汉字学习进行了分析；徐彩华的《汉字认知与汉字学习心理研究》，则专门针对汉字认知进行了分析，运用了大量实验模型和数据统计，结合了心理学和认知科学，对这一领域的研究更加深入和具有前沿性。

第一章　甲级汉字，独体优先

第一节　独体字笔画数少

早在20世纪20年代，我国近现代著名心理学家艾伟就对汉字学习心理进行了研究，考察了文字属性对汉字识别和学习的影响。他以从未学习过汉字的美国大学生为实验对象，要求他们在数秒内观察一个汉字，然后将其默写出来。他发现笔画数在汉字辨认中起着重要作用，即10画以内的汉字容易默写。①

从20年代到八九十年代，许多实验研究都发现，笔画数的多少直接影响着汉字识别的难易程度：字的笔画数越多，识别该字的时间就越长，即笔画数效应。心理学家用眼动技术研究也发现：在阅读中，眼睛注视汉字的时间随着笔画数的增长而增长，笔画数越多，注视时间越长，平均每增加一画，注视时间增加4.6毫秒。

认知心理学家徐彩华通过一系列实验，得出留学生在学习简化字时，在8~9画间出现临界效应：8画以下的汉字比较容易学习，9画（含）以上的汉字对留学生来说难度明显增大。② 在她的实验中，留学生在汉字学习中的笔画数临界点提前了1~2画，这是由于艾伟用于实验的是繁体字，而徐彩华用的是简化字。同时，根据她的研究结论，除学习者自身因素和汉字的课本频率外，笔画数对留学生字形学习影响最大。

通过笔者的统计，在这148个独体字中，有140个字的笔画在8画（含）以下，占总字数的95%左右。只有黄、面、首、须、音、亲、黑、南等8个字在9画（含）以上。也就是说，从笔画数来说，独体字有显著优势，对于留学生来说容易识别、书写，在阅读中所花费的时间也相对较少。

---

① 艾伟．汉字之心理研究．南京：中央大学出版组，1923.

② 徐彩华．汉字认知与汉字学习心理研究．北京：知识产权出版社，2010．226.

第二节　独体字难度系数小

通过实验，徐彩华对《汉语水平词汇与汉字等级大纲》中的 800 个甲级字，从形、音、义三个方面进行了学习难度计算，将 800 个甲级字的学习难度分为较易、中难、较难、高难四个等级。字形学习难度计算，采用笔画数和汉字单音节词频率两个参数，得到字形学习难度等级分布：较难字 184 个，中难字 428 个，较易字 188 个；字音学习难度计算，采用声旁规则性和汉字累计频率两个参数，得到字音学习难度等级分布：高难字 38 个，较难字 66 个，中难字 603 个，较易字 93 个；字义学习难度计算，采用具体性和汉字累计频率两个参数，得到字义学习难度等级分布：较难字 115 个，中难字 580 个，较易字 105 个。根据以上统计结果可以看出，不管是字形、字音还是字义，在 800 个甲级字的学习难度等级分布中，较难字和较易字的数量相当，中难字最多，占到半数以上。

根据徐彩华的实验结果，笔者列出 148 个独体字的学习难度等级分布情况：

148 个独体字	较易	中难	较难	高难
字形	73	65	10	
字音	48	96	3	1
字义	42	100	6	

在这 148 个独体字的学习难度等级分布中，在字形方面，较易字占到了 49% 左右，较难字只占到 6.8% 左右；在字音方面，中难字占到了一半以上，与 800 个甲级字的情况类似，但较难和高难字仅有 4 个，而较易字有 48 个；在字义方面，中难字也占大部分，同样较难字仅有 6 个，而较易字有 42 个。不管是字形、字音还是字义，较难和高难字在这 148 个独体字中只占极少数，远低于 800 个甲级字的平均水平。所以，从学习难度来说，独体字难度系数低，更容易学习。

第三节　独体字能产性高

在汉字形体结构中，有部首、偏旁、部件等说法，三者有重合之处，但性质和作用不尽相同，在这里有必要进行区别和解释。部首指可以成批构字的一部分部件，如以“木”为部首的字有“松、柏、杨、杏、相”等，在字典中通常排在一起，“木”

作为领头单位排在开头，成为查字的依据。所以，部首通常用于辞书编纂或汉字检索领域。偏旁指合体字的构字单位，如“取”字，“耳”和“又”都可以称为其偏旁，而独体字则不存在偏旁。偏旁有时与部首重合，有时不同。部件指由笔画组成的具有组配汉字功能的构字单位，可以与笔画或其他部件再组合，生成其他的合体字或复合结构独体字。只有合体字才有偏旁，但独体字可以有部件。

20 世纪 90 年代，很多学者注意到了部件在汉字教学中的作用。张旺熹在《从汉字部件到汉字结构》中提出：“只要我们在汉字教学的最初阶段，教会学生这 118 个基本部件，那么，学生也就掌握了 1 000 个最常用汉字中的 80% 的部件，无疑，这对于我们的汉字教学，提供了一个很有利的条件。”[①] 2009 年 3 月，教育部和国家语委联合发布了《现代常用字部件及部件名称规范》，通过对 3 500 个常用汉字进行拆分、归纳与统计，确定了 441 组共 514 个部件，同时还确定了 311 个常用的成字部件。所谓成字部件，指可以独立成字的部件，例如“日”字，既可作为部件构成“阳”、“明”等字，又可单独成字。

因为独体字本身已成字，我们只需要再考察这 148 个字中，有多少属于常用部件。通过统计，其中共有 128 个独体字是常用部件，占到了 86% 左右。也就是说，在 148 个独体字中，绝大多数属于常用部件，可以组成其他汉字。同时，通过统计我们还发现，在 3 500 个常用字中，“口”和“日”作为部件分别参与构成了 516 个和 232 个字，构字数排在所有常用部件的前两位。而“一、土、人、十、又、月、女”的构字数也排在前十五位。所以，优先学习这些独体字，对于没有汉语基础的留学生来说，不仅简单易学，而且还为合体字的学习打下了良好的基础，有利于掌握更多的合体字。

另外，我们还对 800 个甲级字中的 652 个合体字做了部件拆分，考察 148 个独体字是否作为部件参与构成这些合体字。拆分方法依据的是《现代常用字部件及部件名称规范》[②] 中的原则。根据统计发现，148 个独体字中有 76 个作为部件参与了 652 个合体字中 319 个的构成，也就是说其中约 49% 的合体字以 76 个独体字作为意符或声符。这进一步说明这些独体字具有很高的能产性。

---

① 张旺熹．从汉字部件到汉字结构——谈对外汉字教学．世界汉语教学，1990（2）．

② 中华人民共和国教育部，国家语言文字工作委员会．现代常用字部件及部件名称规范．北京：语文出版社，2009．2．

第四节　独体字理据性强

文字是记录语言的符号，语言是音义结合的词汇语法体系。用文字记录语言，就是使文字符号与音义建立联系。如果文字与词汇语法体系中的音义有逻辑联系，能够由字形得知字音或字义，我们就认为这种文字符号理据性强；如果文字与词汇语法体系中音义的联系是任意的，不能由字形得知字音或字义，我们认为这种文字符号理据性弱。一般来说，理据性强的文字学习和使用起来较容易，而理据性弱的文字学习和使用起来则较难。

世界上的文字大概分为两种，表音文字和表意文字。不同类型的文字，它的理据性表现方式不同。英语是表音文字，通常可以由音推知形，或由形推知音，甚至如果掌握了一定的词根，还可以由一个词所包含的词根推知词义。汉字通常被认为是表意文字，许慎在《说文解字·叙》中说："象形者，画成其物，随体诘诎……形声者，以事为名，取譬相成……指事者，视而可识，察而见意……会意者，比类合谊，以见指撝"。古汉字中的象形字通常可以由字形推知字义，指事字、会意字、形声字通常可以由其部件推知字义或字音。但是，汉字经过了三千多年的篆化、隶化、楷化、简化甚至到了今天的电脑化，现代汉字的理据性还存在吗？如果存在，是强还是弱，可不可以进行量化分析？这种理据性是否可以运用到对外汉字教学中？这些问题，都是我们必须思考和解决的。

为了对汉字的理据性进行量化，苏培成在《现代汉字学纲要》中提出了"理据度"的概念①。他从构字法上把现代汉字分成六类：会意字、形声字、半意符半记号字、半音符半记号字、独体记号字、合体记号字。理据度是指意符、音符在全部字符中所占的比例。理据度的计算公式是：

实际具有的理据值÷可能具有的最大理据值＝理据度

他把一、二两类字的理据值记为10，称为有理据字；三、四两类字的理据值记为5，称为半理据字；五、六两类字的理据值记为0，称为无理据字。他以《新华字典》里的"又"、"冫"、"刂"、"鱼"四个部首下面的字来做抽样测查，结果得出："又"部首下有27个字，其中理据字是6个，半理据字是4个，无理据字是17个，"又"部首统摄的字实际理据值是80，最大理据值是270，理据度是0.29；"鱼"部首统摄

① 苏培成．现代汉字学纲要．北京：北京大学出版社，2001．103—104．

的字理据度是0.86。

苏培成的计算方法，是将某个部首作为意符或音符能否在合体字中表明字义或字音作为判断条件，得出以这个部首为构件的合体字的整体理据度。而我们则希望考察独体字本身是否能表明字义或字音，其理据度是高还是低。

张和生在《基于二语教学的汉字构形理据量化研究》① 中对《汉语水平词汇与汉字等级大纲》的汉字也进行了理据度的分析，他在苏培成的基础上采用了不尽相同的测量尺度。首先，他将汉字基本分为象形、指事、会意、形声四类。对于象形、指事两类，采用字形回溯的方式分析其理据度；对于会意字，则采用偏旁义相加求得字义的方式计算其理据度；对于形声字，他的计算方法则大致与苏培成的方法相同，只是所选择的部首数量更多，其构成的形声字范围更广。

我们主要希望考察独体字本身所具有的理据性是强还是弱，其理据度大概是多少。因此，打算采用张和生的方法，首先将148个独体字按象形、指事、会意、形声进行分类。

因为象形、指事、会意还有形声等分类，主要是判断字形、字义、字音三者之间存在怎样的联系。但是，汉字的字形、字音、字义，经过三千多年的发展也在不断发生着变化。所以在进行分类之前，我们首先要解决两个问题：一是以什么字形为标准，二是以什么字义为标准。如果不解决这两个问题，在分类时可能会产生混乱，有的字在甲骨文中是象形字，在金文或小篆中却是会意字。

象形、指事、会意、形声是中国传统汉字理论“六书”中的四种。“六书”最早出现在《周礼》中，但其中只有“六书”之名，而无具体解释。后来班固、郑众和许慎各自列出了“六书”的名目和顺序，但班固和郑众也没有做具体解释，只有许慎对他所列出的“六书”的每个条例分别做了说明，但是也比较笼统。在这里，我们采用高明在《中国古文字学通论》② 中的说法：象形字是指按照客观事物的形体，随其圆转曲直描绘出的一种具有形象感的代表符号，以表达语言中的词义；指事字是指在用象形的方法难以表示事物特点的时候，利用标注记号的方法指出所表示事物的要点，即在两个符号中，一个是字，另一个是符号；会意字是由两个或两个以上的符号组成，以图形的组合或符号的意义组合构成新的词义。根据汉字发展规律，象形字、指事字和会意字是较早的文字，现代汉字中几乎已经没有了，因此，用现代汉字字形来进行这种分类就没有什么意义。所以，我们在对148个独体字进行分类时，主要是依据它们的甲骨文字形，字义则是根据当时所使用的字义。对于少数没有甲骨文字形

---

① 张和生．基于二语教学的汉字构形理据量化研究．北京师范大学学报（社会科学版），2011（6）．

② 高明．中国古文字学通论．北京：北京大学出版社，1996．47—50．

的字，如“飞”、“互”、“亲”等，如果有金文字形则依据金文字形，如果没有则依据小篆字形，字义都是依据所选用字形当时的字义。对于一些字形与字义已不符的字，也是就说字形所表示的本义已不用或不明，主要是用作假借字，例如“我”、“不”、“其”等，则归入“无法分类”一栏。

148 类型	字数	
象形	67	才、车、大、单、刀、电、冬、儿、而、方、飞、干、工、公、果、互、户、回、火、几、交、角、斤、口、了、力、马、毛、门、米、母、目、牛、女、齐、气、且、求、人、日、肉、山、舍、身、生、示、世、手、首、水、太、午、心、辛、行、幸、羊、衣、用、又、鱼、月、乐、云、子、自、足
指事	24	本、必、二、丰、夫、面、民、千、三、上、少、术、四、天、下、向、小、须、一、尤、元、支、中、主
会意	28	半、出、非、父、共、合、黑、会、介、久、开、老、立、亲、声、束、为、文、言、音、永、雨、正、之、走、见、长、页
无法分类	29	八、白、百、不、厂、弟、东、个、黄、己、今、九、来、两、六、么、南、片、平、七、其、十、万、我、五、西、也、巳、广

根据以上分类，可以看出这些独体字中，象形字占到45%，指事字占到16%，会意字占到19%，无法分类的字占到20%。也就是说，148个独体字在古文字阶段，80%具有很强的理据性，可以通过字形看出字义。

那么这些独体字在现代汉语中，理据性的强弱又是怎样的呢？我们再利用张和生的方法，对这些字进行理据度的分析。对于象形字和指事字，通过字形回溯分析理据度，也就是说通过它们的古汉字字形（小篆、金文、甲骨文等），看是否能把握和领会它们在现代汉语中的字义。如果可以直接领会，则定为“透明”；如果要通过讲解才能领会，则定为“半透明”；如果经讲解后仍难以领会，则定为“不透明”。对于会意字，如果通过偏旁义相加就可以比较清楚地体现该字在现代汉语中的字义，则定为形义关系“透明”；如果通过偏旁义相加后需要加以解释才可辗转体现字义的，则定为形义关系“半透明”；如果通过偏旁义相加后经解释仍不能体现字义的，则定为形义关系“不透明”。需要说明的是，这些字在现代汉语中的字义有很多，这里主要是指《汉语大字典》中的最常用义。还有一点需要指出的是，我们通过界定形义关系的“透明”、“半透明”和“不透明”来对汉字的理据度进行判断，在具体的操作中难免存在一定的主观性。

	透明	半透明	不透明
象形	车、刀、飞、火、角、口、马、毛、门、米、目、牛、人、日、山、手、水、心、羊、衣、鱼、月、云、足	大、电、儿、果、户、回、交、力、母、女、气、肉、舍、生、首、太、行、乐、子	才、单、冬、而、方、干、工、公、互、几、斤、了、齐、且、求、身、示、世、午、辛、幸、用、又、自
指事	本、二、三、四、一、中	夫、面、民、上、少、天、下、小、元、支、	必、丰、千、术、向、须、尤、主
会意	开、老、雨、走、见	半、出、非、父、合、黑、会、立、束、为、言、音、长	共、介、亲、声、文、永、正、之、页、久

从上表可以看出，在67个象形字中，透明字24个，半透明字19个，不透明字24个；在24个指事字中，透明字6个，半透明字10个，不透明字8个；在28个会意字中，透明字5个，半透明字13个，不透明字10个。在这119个字中，透明字一共35个，半透明字42个，不透明字42个。如果加上不能分类的29个字，不透明字是71个，占48%，透明和半透明字是77个，占52%。

通过以上数据分析得出，这148个独体字的理据性较强，可以通过字形回溯领会字义的占一半以上。这种理据性如果不在汉语字词教学当中加以利用，可以说是忽略了汉字的特色，是一种教学资源的浪费。张和生在《基于二语教学的汉字构形理据量化研究》中说：“可以肯定的是，汉字构形理据是重要的教学资源。无论是哪种汉字教学模式，都可以通过讲授汉字构形知识的方法来强化教学效果。”

根据以上论证，可以得出独体字具有以下特点：笔画简单，方便掌握；难度系数低，易于学习；能产性高，绝大多数属于常用部件，可参与构成大量合体字，为留学生进一步学习合体字打下基础；理据性强，利于学习，能增强学习者兴趣。所以，我们从800个甲级字中，筛选出其中的148个独体字优先学习，具有一定的科学依据。

但同时我们也应该注意到，汉字在发展变化的过程中，其理据度是逐渐减弱的。在甲骨文时代，这148个字可以说有80%具有很强的理据性，但在现代汉语中，只有52%具有理据性，其中有28%还需要通过字形回溯加以讲解，才能将形与义联系起来。所以，这就需要我们在汉字教材中采用一定的方法，来利用并加强汉字的这种理据性。因此，我们提出了图画开路和精选古文字字形的方法，将在下文具体论述。

第二章　图画开路，源头体现

第一节　图画具有趣味性

对于具有拼音文字背景的留学生来说，汉字字形结构复杂，难以认识和记忆，学生由此产生畏难情绪，认为汉字枯燥难学。其实，字形是汉字与拼音文字最大的不同之处。汉字字形，特别是古文字字形，如甲骨文、金文等，在造字之初就具有很强的图画性。如果不将汉字这一可贵的特性运用在教学里，岂不枉费了汉字最初以图形表意的本质？因此，利用这一特点，我们为这些汉字一一配上图片，用图画简单明了、直观地描绘出具体事物，可以大大增加学习的趣味性，从而吸引学生的注意力。同时，研究也表明，视觉表象在记忆过程中起重要作用，“给学习者呈现图画材料，或者要求学习者对记忆材料进行想象、在大脑中形成鲜明的视觉意象，都会促进学习者的记忆”①。

在这方面，很多学者做了有益尝试。如陈火平的《趣味汉字》、熊国英的《图释古汉字》、张惠芬的《张老师教汉字·汉字识写课本》、佟大汶的《图解汉字》等，在讲解汉字时都配上了相应的图片，并且“这些图片描写的是几千年很少变化的事物，是操任何母语、在任何年龄段的学习者都容易看懂的世界性语言”②。

第二节　图画体现古汉字的源头

在文字产生之前，人们通常用图画来记事或传递信息，这些图画称为文字画。文字产生之后，仍然有较多文字具有很强的图画性，例如金文中用来记录国族名号的氏

① 江新．对外汉语教学的心理学探索．北京：教育科学出版社，2007．73．

② 曹兆兰．《外国人识字卡》编写探索．第十届双语双方言研讨会论文选集．深圳：深圳报业集团出版社，2011．23．

族徽号——"（目）"、"（耳）"等，还有至今仍在使用的纳西文字中的东巴文，如"（石）"、"（夜）"等，都具有很浓厚的图画特点，字形以象物、象事或象意为主。但与图画不同的是，图画的目的在于追求美感、惟妙惟肖，而文字的目的在于记录事物、表达情感，图画只是一种载体。所以，不管是文字产生之前还是之后，图画都与之有着千丝万缕、难以割舍的联系。特别是在古文字阶段，这种联系表现得更紧密，如甲骨文中的"（山）"，金文中的"（日）"、"（月）"等，都是用图形来表示事物，我们把这类文字称为象形字。

而根据第一章第四节的统计，148 个独体字在古文字阶段，有 45% 是象形字、16% 是指事字、19% 是会意字。这些字配上图画，不仅可以清楚地体现其字源，还可以与本书《识字卡》中的甲骨文、金文字形等古文字字形一起，展现汉字产生、发展的完整体系，建立起字形与字义之间的联系。吕必松在论述汉字教学时，就提倡"用实物或图片解释字义"的方法。他指出："用这种方法解释字义，简单明了，又可以加快建立声音和概念的直接联系，因此凡是能够用实物或图片解释的，应当尽量用实物或图片。"①

① 吕必松．汉语和汉语作为第二语言教学．北京：北京大学出版社，2007．167．

第三章　字形精选，展示演变

第一节　汉字的性质

关于汉字的性质，学界有诸多说法，总结起来主要有以下三种观点：有人认为汉字是表意体系的文字[①]，汉字主要是用大量不同笔画构成的表意符号来记录汉语的语素，用不同的字形来区别不同的语素或者词。现在仍有很多学者持这种观点，如郑振峰、王军、李彦循、唐健雄等；有人认为汉字是意音文字，因为现代汉字的90%是形声字，而形声字是用形旁表意、声旁表音，所以，汉字是“综合运用表意兼表音两种表达方法”的“意音文字”[②]；裘锡圭认为，“一种文字的性质应该是由这种文字所使用的符号的性质决定的”[③]，汉字是记录汉语的符号，而汉字的书写形式是汉字的符号，因为汉字的书写形式中有大量意符、音符和记号，所以汉字主要有三种类型：表意字（象形字、指事字、会意字）、表音字（假借字）、半表意半表音字（形声字），还有一小部分记号、半记号字。

三种观点各有道理，在这里我们不讨论哪种说法更合理，但从中我们可以得出：有相当一部分汉字（象形字、指事字、会意字、形声字）具有表意功能，其字形能够体现字源或字义。但是现代汉字由于字形演变，已较难从字形一眼看出其表示的意义，所以需要列出甲骨文、金文、小篆等古文字字形，以展示汉字的演变。

第二节　汉字字形演变特点及趋势

汉字的发展历经三千多年，从最初的甲骨文、金文，到小篆、隶书，再到行书、

① 黄伯荣，廖序东．现代汉语．北京：高等教育出版社，2002．164．

② 周有光．文字演进的一般规律．中国语文，1957（7）．

③ 裘锡圭．文字学概要．北京：商务印书馆，2010．10．

楷书，虽然总体而言仍然是方块字，但是不同时期的汉字，形体上却有不同的特点，并且产生了较大的变化。

甲骨文和金文是早期汉字，字体具有很强的图画性，也就是说象形度高。需要指出的是，金文并不是在甲骨文的基础上顺承延续的。两者有三百多年的共时，所使用的场合、目的、材料以及书写手法有很大不同，因此两者的形体也体现出不同的特点。

甲骨文主要是记录商王朝统治者的占卜事宜，金文在商代也已出现，但全盛时代是在西周，主要是记录周王朝统治者、贵族大臣等的赏赐册命、颂扬君恩、祭典训诰等内容。商王朝的占卜很多，是否下雨、战争是否取胜、生孩子是否顺利、农业是否丰收等，都是占卜的内容，因此甲骨文的使用场合很多；青铜器在商周时期是贵重物品，代表着尊贵的地位和财富，一般是在举行仪式时使用。甲骨文刻在龟甲或兽骨上，所使用的书写工具是刻刀之类；金文是铸造在青铜器上的文字，使用铸和刻两种方法，早期的金文主要是与青铜器一起铸成，战国时期的金文，有的是在铜器铸成后刻上去的。下面我们把一些甲骨文和金文字形列出来，进行对比。

现代汉字	又	月	父	且	子
甲骨文	（粹 194）	（粹 659）	（铁 196.1）	（甲 249）	（后下 42.7）
金文（商代或西周早期）	（利簋）	（我方鼎）	（隻妇父庚卣盖）	（日祖壬爵）	（子作妇婳彝）
金文（西周中晚期）	（虢季子白盘）	（虢季子白盘）	（毛公鼎）	（散氏盘）	（𢦚簋）

从以上字形大概可以看出，甲骨文和早期金文象形度都很高，但两者也有区别：甲骨文笔画较硬，金文笔画较圆润。到了西周中晚期，金文字形趋向整齐方正，笔画趋向线条化、平直化，从“子”字的变化可以明显看出。

小篆一般被认为是秦始皇统一六国后，推行“书同文”政策，在秦系文字的基础上经过整理产生的文字，是当时所使用的“正体”文字。秦朝虽然在历史上寿命很短，但是它所推行的文字改革运动，却对汉字的发展产生了深远的影响。经过规范整理，使汉字基本走向定型。

隶书产生于秦朝，被认为是“起于官狱”，是为了应付当时繁忙的官狱事务而造的一种简便字体，因为施之于奴隶，所以得名“隶书”，是当时所用的“俗体”文字。从字形来说，小篆复杂，隶书简单；从笔画来说，小篆圆转，隶书方折。下面我们将举例说明。

现代汉字	利	黑	信	河	路
小篆	利	黑	信	河	路
隶书	利	黑	信	河	路

从上面的例子可以大概看出，隶书字形与小篆有较大不同，偏旁大大简化，如“黑”下部的“火”，在隶书中简化为“灬”，“河”的偏旁“水”，在隶书中简化为“氵”。这些简化偏旁后来被固定下来，一直沿用至今。隶书虽然在当时是俗体，但是随着社会的发展，文字的使用越来越频繁，书写方便的隶书更符合人们的需求，因此到了西汉，隶书正式取代了小篆，成为主要字体。

我们再来看看楷书的兴起和特点。对于楷书，裘锡圭在《文字学概要》中说：“大约在汉魏之际，又在行书的基础上形成了楷书。楷书出现后，隶书和新隶体并没有很快就丧失它们的地位。经过魏晋时代长达二百年左右的时间，楷书才最终发展成为占统治地位的主要字体。”① 下面我们通过字形对比，来看看隶书与楷书的区别。

现代汉字	利	被	然	因	驾
隶书	利	被	然	因	駕
楷书	利	被	然	因	駕

从上面的例子可以看出，隶书到楷书的发展变化过程中，有的偏旁进一步简化，笔画出现捺笔和硬钩，例如，“利”的偏旁“刀”，在隶书中还能看出刀的形状，到了楷书则简化成“刂”，笔画出现硬钩，“被”的偏旁“衣”，在楷书中被简化成“衤”；字形也进一步简化，例如，隶书中“驾”的偏旁“马”下面的四点，到楷书中被简化成一横。楷书的字形进一步简化，形体更加注重对称，笔画出现硬钩，象形性逐渐减弱，越来越趋向现代汉字的符号化特点。

① 裘锡圭．文字学概要．北京：商务印书馆，2010．74．

第三节 字形显示字义，展现演变

一、字形显示字义

早在20世纪初期，一些近现代心理学家就已发现字形对理解字义的作用很大，如刘廷芳（1891—1947）用联想学习的观点考察了汉字的心理特点，从而发现字形对理解字义的作用大于字音对理解字义的作用。艾伟通过考察汉字形、音、义的联想特点，发现“形—义”联想比“形—音”联想更持久；字形呈现后，解释字义比不解释字义保持得更持久。这说明，字形的掌握对字义的掌握有很大作用，两者相互影响、相互促进。在讲解汉字时，有必要解释字义；在解释字义时，也必须给出字形。

在第一章第四节的论述中，我们计算出在148个独体字中，有35个字通过字形回溯，能直接体现字义，有42个字通过字形回溯及适当讲解，可以辗转体现字义。因此，要想利用这些字的理据性，就必须列出它们的古文字字形，这样才能把汉字字形与字义联系起来，才能让学习者通过字形理解字义。

吕必松在论述汉字教学策略时也提到：“因为汉字有直观表义的特点，所以可以根据字形解释字义。根据字形解释字义，目的是帮助学生理解和记忆汉字。”① 本书《识字卡》所选的独体字大多为象形字、指事字或会意字，根据前面的计算，其中24%具有直观表义性，28%具有间接表义性，所以我们将这些字的古代字形都一一列出，以直观地建立起字形与字义的联系。

二、字形有利于培养学生的汉字结构意识

文字识别的主要目的是理解文字的意义，那么在意义提取过程中，语音和字形分别起怎样的作用呢？现代认知心理学研究发现，对于具有拼音文字（如英语）背景的人来说，在阅读过程中提取文字的意义有三种可能：一是字形激活字音，字音通达意义，即通达途径是形—音—义；二是字形直接激活意义；三是存在双通道可能，即上面两种通达途径都存在。但是大多数研究者认为，语音通路即使不是意义通达的唯一

① 吕必松．汉语和汉语作为第二语言教学．北京：北京大学出版社，2007．166．

途径，也是最重要的途径，而由形到义的通路即使存在，也是次要的。

对于具有汉语背景的人来说，提取意义的通路是否也与英语一样呢？目前学界也有不同看法：Perfetti C. A.（帕费迪）通过一系列研究提出，汉语和英语一样，语音在意义通达中起主要作用，没有语音就不能激活意义；周晓林认为，对于意义的激活，语音的作用是有限的，而从形到义的激活更为迅速有效，在汉字加工中，“语音信息的激活并不比语义信息早，语音激活也不是语义激活的先决条件”①；徐彩华也认为，在强调词义的任务中，字形对词义的激活很重要也很迅速，此时语音也可能被自动激活，但其对词义通达的贡献有限。

我们认为汉语和英语在提取意义时究竟采用哪种通道、是否一样，可能并不在于两种语言本身的区别，至少这不是主要原因，或许更多是因为读者的不同文字背景。

对于拼音文字背景的读者来说，在他们的心理词典中，字义跟字音相关更紧密。而在汉字背景的读者中，字义跟字形的关联则更为密切。江新在实验中就发现：“有表意文字背景的日韩学生记忆汉字的意义可能不依赖汉字的正确读音，而有表音文字背景的印度尼西亚、美国学生记忆汉字的意义则可能依赖汉字的读音。”②

以上研究及实验结果对我们的对外汉字教学有两点启发：第一，对外汉字教学要注重字音的教学；第二，除了重视字音外，更重要的是培养留学生的汉字结构意识，让他们对汉字字形有整体的了解和感性的认识，从而在头脑中建立起字形与字义的联系。这是因为在汉语普通话中，只有410多个音节，而仅国家语委发布的常用汉字就有3 500个。音节少而字形多，导致汉语中同音字很多。随着留学生识字量的增加，仅靠有限字音难以区别大量的意义，必须通过掌握大量的字形才能区别意义。

因此，本书《识字卡》一一列出了甲骨文、金文、小篆、楷书等汉字字形。这样，不管是从人脑加工汉字的过程来说，还是从汉字本身的特点来说，都有助于对字义的掌握。

三、字形展现演变

本书在《识字卡》中列出各种字形的目的还在于展示汉字的演变。汉字的发展演变至少有几千年的历史，从早期的甲骨文、金文到后来的楷书，每个字的字形少则数十，多则上千，这就需要对字形进行挑选从而更好地展示其演变。“《识字卡》的目的

---

① 周晓林，曲延轩，庄捷．再探汉字加工中语音、语义激活的相对时间进程．心理与行为研究，2003(4)．

② 江新．对外汉语教学中的心理学探索．北京：教育科学出版社，2007．113．

不是教外国人学习古汉字，只是通过古汉字，达到认识楷书、掌握词汇的目的。”[①] 所以《识字卡》选字的原则是：图画开路、楷书压阵，中间挑选汉字演变过程中有代表性的字体，如甲骨文、金文、小篆、隶书等。如果帛书、草书、行书等辅助字体对某些汉字的演变产生了重要作用，则也会列出。总之，“与演变有‘直系’关系的入选，与演变仅有‘旁系’关系的一律不选。”[②]

目前所知，金文并不比甲骨文出现的时间晚。由于材质、目的与方法的不同，青铜器上所铸的金文，有些相比甲骨上所刻的甲骨文字形，象形程度更高、更生动逼真，显示了更古的文字面貌。也就是说，有些金文字形与图画更为接近。所以，按照“展示演变”的原则，本《识字卡》有时会将金文字形列在甲骨文的前面。

小篆字形上承金文、下接隶书，是秦始皇统一六国后在全国范围内使用的文字，也是古文字和今文字之间的分界点，在汉字字形的发展演变中占据着重要的地位。因此，《识字卡》中的文字，我们除了列出甲骨文、金文外，还列出了小篆字形。

另外，在第二节我们论述过，为了方便书写，秦代的人民群众在小篆之外，还创造了俗体文字——隶书，因此有的字形在隶书中变化很大，并且这种变化后的字形一直沿用至今。对于这种情况，我们也列出了相应的隶书字形，以体现汉字字形演变发展的连续性。

对于楷书字形，《识字卡》分两种情况处理：如果楷书与简体字字形一致，则直接列出楷书；如果不一致，也就是说楷书繁体字字形与简体字字形不一致，则也在《识字卡》中列出繁体字字形。

同时，《识字卡》在楷书简体的下面，还列出了该字的笔顺。笔顺对于非汉字文化圈的初学者来说非常重要，这也是一个不可缺少的环节。

---

① 曹兆兰.《外国人识字卡》编写探索. 第十届双语双方言研讨会论文选集. 深圳：深圳报业集团出版社，2011. 24.

② 曹兆兰.《外国人识字卡》编写探索. 第十届双语双方言研讨会论文选集. 深圳：深圳报业集团出版社，2011. 25.

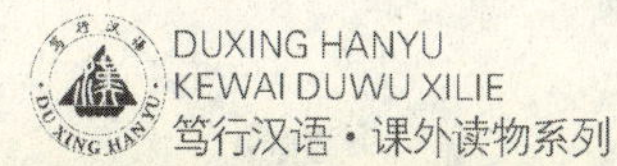

第四节　古文字字形承载了中国文化

一、历史悠久

汉字字体的演变，一般分为两个阶段：一是古文字阶段，起自商代，终于秦代，字体包括甲骨文、金文、帛书、小篆等；二是今文字阶段，起自汉代，延续至今，字体包括隶书、草书、行书、楷书等。

大多数古文字学家认为，甲骨文是我国目前所能看到的最早且比较完备的文字。既然已经比较完备，那么在此之前必然有一个较长的发展阶段。历史学家和古文字学家郭沫若曾认为我国文字的产生可以一直追溯到六千年前的半坡仰韶文化。他认为半坡陶钵口沿上刻的二三十种符号应该就是汉字的原始阶段。对于这一观点，目前学术界还有争议。我们在这里暂且搁置争议，在没有形成确定说法的情况下，仍将甲骨文看作汉字的开端。

1899 年，甲骨文被发现于河南省安阳市小屯村，也就是商代都朝的遗址——殷墟。甲骨文是刻在龟甲或兽骨上的文字，目前已知的最早的甲骨文大约是公元前 14 世纪的文字，距今约三千五百年。在已经发现的商代后期的文字资料里，甲骨文最多，其次就是金文。金文是铸造在青铜器上的文字。因材料、书写方式、目的不同而与甲骨文相区别，但在使用时间上，金文的出现并不比甲骨文晚，两者至少有三百年的共时。也就是说，早在三千多年前，殷人已开始用甲骨文记录占卜事宜，用金文记录器主族名、祭祀战事等。

世界上的很多文字，包括后面将要提到的埃及圣体文、苏美尔楔形文字等，最初都跟汉字一样具有表意的性质。后来随着语言的发展，表意文字已不能满足表达复杂语言的需要，而渐渐消亡或转为表音文字。汉字也有表音的趋向，比如后来出现的大量形声字，它们的声符主要就是用来表音的。但需要指出的是，汉字并没有完全表音化，也不是拼音文字，仍然是以笔画为基础的，主要以字形来区别意义。从甲骨文、金文、小篆、隶书到楷书，汉字虽历经三千多年的发展，却没有发生本质的改变。

二、体系完整

甲骨文被大多数文字学家公认为是比较完备的文字形式。目前，已经挖掘出土的甲骨大约有十多万片。从数量上来说，甲骨文中出现的单字数量已达4 000多字，已经识别确定的有1 000多个，而根据国家语委和教育部1988年发布的《现代汉语常用字表》，我们目前的常用字也才3 500个；从造字方法来说，甲骨文中已经出现象形字、指事字、会意字、假借字和形声字，例如：水——（象形），上——（指事），休——（会意），不——（假借），洋——（形声），这些造字方法包括了汉字的基本造字方法；从词汇方面说，甲骨文中已经出现了名词、动词、形容词、代词、数词、副词等大多数实词种类，如："翌癸未勿燎五牛。"（《合》12051正）大意是，在将来的癸未日不宜用五头牛举行燎祭。这句卜辞中，出现了名词"牛"、动词"燎"（一种祭祀方法）、数词"五"、副词"勿"。又如："癸卯卜，㱿，贞：我不其受年。"（《合》9710）大意是，癸卯日占卜，㱿问：我商王朝将不会获得好年成吗？这句卜辞中，出现了代词"我"。又如："勿呼多子逐鹿。"（《合》乙3083）大意是，不要号令众王子公子追捕鹿。这句卜辞中，出现了形容词"多"。

除了大多数实词已经具备，还有不少虚词如介词、语气词，甲骨文也已经使用。从记载的内容来说，甲骨文所记录的内容极为丰富，涉及商代社会生活的诸多方面，不仅包括政治、军事、文化、社会习俗等内容，而且涉及天文、历法、医药等科学技术，这里不再一一举例。

金文的字数，据容庚《金文编》记载，共计3 772个，其中可以识别的字有2 420个。殷商时期的青铜器上大多只有寥寥数字，多为族名、享祭者名或作器者名，最长的铭文也只有40多字。到了西周时期，金文进入全盛时代，篇幅长达百字以上的铭文屡见不鲜，如西周前期的大盂鼎有291字，后期的散氏盘有350字，毛公鼎有498字，这些铭文记叙清晰、语言流畅、结构完整。金文所记内容也是丰富多彩的，"在大量的青铜器铭文中，记载着王室政治谋划、君王后妃事迹、祭典训诰、宴飨田猎、征伐方国、赏赐册命、奴隶买卖、刑事诉讼、盟誓契约、家史婚媾等，都是反映当时社会的政治、经济、军事、法制、礼仪情况的重要资料，具有明确的史书性质。"①

① 曹兆兰．金文与殷周女性文化．北京：北京大学出版社，2004．9．

三、字形优美

郭沫若在《殷契粹编》的序言中，就对甲骨文的书体风格非常赞赏："卜辞契于龟骨，其契之精而字之美，每令吾辈数千载后人神往。文字作风且因人因世而异，大抵武丁之世，字多雄浑，帝乙之世，文咸秀丽。而行之疏密，字之结构，回环照应，井井有条……足知现存契文，实一代法书，而书之契之者，乃殷世之钟王颜柳也。"①

甲骨文一般是用刀直接在龟甲兽骨上刻字，所以刀法能真实地体现作者笔意。甲骨文的笔画通常犀利有劲、各有特色；线条有粗有细、有长有短；结构一般呈瘦长形，有大小、长短、方圆之别；字形变化多样，可向左可向右、可倒写可侧写，并无定式；风格古拙朴素，无雕琢修饰，充满自然古朴之美。

同时，甲骨文中的刻辞排列也很有规律，或从右至左，或从左至右，或从中间分至两边、左右对称。一片甲骨上少则数字，多则上百字。其章法布置毫不做作、错落自然。无论从哪方面看，都体现了殷代刻手们——也就是郭沫若所说的"殷世之钟王颜柳"，朴拙自然的艺术技巧和艺术匠心。所以，甲骨文不愧为中国最早的书法艺术。

金文是铸刻在青铜器上的文字，由于材料、方法、用途的不同，其整体风格又与甲骨文有所区别。如果说甲骨文是当时所用的"俗体"，体现了古拙、朴素、自然的风格，那么金文则是当时所用的"正体"，表现出端庄、精美、大气的特点。

西周时期的金文是一种很成熟的书法艺术，向来受到书法史家的重视。金文早在汉代就已被发现，宋代文人欧阳修、赵明诚也都对此作过研究和记载。长期以来，人们普遍认为，谈书法只能从隶书、楷书开始，只有魏晋南北朝以后才有真正的书法艺术。而金文改变了这种传统认识，将中国书法艺术的历史至少可以推溯至三千年前。

从字体来说，金文的特点是"肥、实、圆"。金文好用肥笔，字体经常填实，笔道圆滑；从铭文排列结构来说，大多由右至左、竖行排列，字距安排合理。以《毛公鼎》为例，其铭文的字体整齐遒丽、结构严整、瘦劲流畅，布局不驰不急、行止得当，历来被众多书法家或爱好者作为摹写范本。此外，上文提到的《大盂鼎》、《散氏盘》铭文也被认为是金文中的上乘之作。

秦始皇统一六国后，推行"书同文、车同轨"的政策，于是小篆就成为统一使用的文字。首先，我们有必要对小篆作一些解释。许慎在《说文解字》中提到"斯作《仓颉篇》，中车府令赵高作《爰历篇》，太史令胡毋敬作《博学篇》，皆取史籀大篆，

① 郭沫若．殷契粹编·序言．北京：科学出版社，1965．10—11．

或颇省改，所谓小篆者也”[①]，他认为小篆是李斯等人在大篆的基础上，进行改造而制定出的一种字体。而通过对古文字资料的考证，裘锡圭认为：“小篆是由春秋战国时代的秦国文字逐渐演变而成的，不是由籀文‘省改’而成的。”[②] 因为许慎所处时代的局限性，他没有见到甲骨文，对金文、战国文字等文字资料也接触不多，无法进行科学的对比考证，所以说法有失妥当。并且，根据马克思的唯物主义观点，某一种通用的文字形式必定不是由某一人创造的。所以，本文采用裘锡圭的说法，认为小篆是由秦国文字演变而来的。

文字发展到小篆阶段，字形进一步趋于规整匀称。与甲骨文、金文等相比，象形意味逐渐削弱。同时，由于统一文字、便于交流的需要，字形方向、偏旁位置不固定的现象，在小篆中也显著减少。

小篆字形优美，线条粗细一致，匀称大方；字体端庄严谨，疏密得当；结构布局合理，从容平和；章法行列整齐，规矩和谐。因此，历来受到众多书法家的青睐。同时，由于其特有的形式美，在现代社会中也被广泛地应用，如在现代建筑、娱乐游戏、大学校徽、现代教育、创意产业及日常生活中，都不乏小篆的身影。并且，由于小篆笔画复杂、形式奇古，可以随意添加曲折，因此在印章刻制上，尤其是需要防伪的官方印章，也多采用篆书。

四、生命力强

人类文明史上起源最早的文字，目前公认的有两河流域的苏美尔楔形文字、尼罗河流域的埃及圣体文、中国的汉字和中美洲的玛雅文字。楔形文字和圣体文早在两千多年前就已经消亡，直到 18 世纪才被破解。虽然中美洲的玛雅印第安人至今仍能说玛雅语，但其文字早在 16 世纪就成为了死文字。目前，只有中国的汉字是唯一连续使用三千多年并且仍在使用的文字。

从自身来说，汉字的发展历程并非一帆风顺，其中也经受了各种考验。例如，在中国历史上，蒙古人曾入主中原，建立了大元王朝。蒙古人有自己的语言和文字，并且在统治时期推行蒙语、蒙文。然而，直到蒙古统治结束，汉语和汉字的地位也未能被撼动。到了近代，在新文化运动时期，又有一批知识分子主张废除汉字，认为与拼音文字相比，汉字落后且复杂。20 世纪 50 年代，还出现过将汉字改为拼音文字的主

---

① 许慎. 说文解字·叙. 上海：上海教育出版社，2003. 1.

② 裘锡圭. 文字学概要. 北京：商务印书馆，2010. 64.

张，甚至得到一大批文字学家如唐兰，语言学家如周有光、吕叔湘等人的支持和赞同。然而，汉字仍然以其广大的使用基础和顽强的生命力，经受住了各种挑战，顺利进入21世纪。

从字形来说，虽然汉字经历了从甲骨文、金文、篆书到隶书、楷书的不断演变，但其根本性质并没有改变，仍然是方块字，横平竖直；仍然具有表意性质，与拼音文字有显著区别；且甲骨文、金文的一些象形字，字形发展至今也并无太大变化，如"[illegible]（大）"、"[illegible]（口）"、"[illegible]（日）"、"[illegible]（月）"等。我们目前仍在使用汉字，也未见给书写以及电脑输入带来任何不便。所以，有理由相信，汉字必将继续使用下去，至少在可以预见的未来，不会被其他文字所取代。

第五节　字形典故能有效提高学习兴趣

通过对外国人汉字学习策略使用的调查，江新、赵果发现：在各种汉语学习动机中，"汉字圈"学生由于将来职业的需要而引发的汉语学习动机最强，"非汉字圈"学生对于汉语感兴趣而引发的汉语学习动机最强。① 而我们的《识字卡》正好是针对"非汉字圈"的学生，那么在学习中如何提升他们对汉语、汉字的兴趣，是我们要考虑和关注的问题之一。

对于汉字初学者来说，汉字的笔画结构、表意特点等，都使他们兴味盎然，同时又感觉神秘莫测。因为这是一种与拼音文字截然不同的文字，它不是由字母而是由笔画组成，不是线性结构而是方块结构，不是表音而是表意。它古老而又现代，传承了中国几千年的文明，并且顺利进入了信息时代。它的造字原理和发展历史，体现着中国人独特的哲学观和世界观。对于他们来说，了解和掌握汉字，相当于从另一个角度去看世界。"而提升学生兴趣的最基本途径，就是站在中外文化比较的交汇点上，对汉字的造字理据进行文化的阐释，把汉字形成的自然、社会、历史、文化背景生动地展示给学生。"②

例如，"生"这个字，甲骨文和金文中，字形像一棵小草破土而出、生根发芽，最下面的一横即代表"地面"。草木破土而出是"生"，那么人来到世界也称为"生"，后来变成双音词"生育"。新的东西制作出来了，也叫"生"，即"生产"。再

① 江新．对外汉语教学的心理学探索．北京：教育科学出版社，2007．119．

② 欧阳祯人．对外汉字教学的文化透视．北京：北京大学出版社，2009．145．

如“先”这个字，在甲骨文和金文中，字形是“[illegible]”，上部是人的一只脚，下部是一个人。“脚”走到“人”前面去了，这就是“先”。

这些字形的解释和典故生动有趣，能有效提高初学者对汉字的学习兴趣和热情。同时，也具有相当的科学性，得到了学界的普遍认同，并不是作者凭空想象出来，生搬硬套到字形上去的。

第四章　阐述字义，英语解释

第一节　阐述字义

本《识字卡》是针对“非汉字文化圈”学生而设计的汉字学习资料，让初学者更方便快捷地掌握汉字字形是我们的愿望，但绝非终极目标。我们的目标是，通过《识字卡》，让学习者整体掌握汉字形、音、义三方面的内容，从而能够正确使用汉字进行有效交流。

汉字的学习，绝不能将形、音、义割裂开来孤立进行。忽视单个汉字与汉字系统之间的联系，忽视字形和字音、字义之间的联系，就是“只看树木、不见森林”，这种方法必然不能取得好的学习效果。所以，在给出汉字字形时，有必要同时给出字音、阐释字义，让学生在三者之间建立起统一的联系。

因此，《识字卡》对每个字都给出了简明扼要的解释。独体字大多是象形字、指事字或会意字，并且一半以上具有表意的特点。所以，我们首先是回溯甲骨文、金文等古文字字形，通过字形引出本义，本义就是“造字之初准备让它表示的意思，通常也就是作为造字对象的词在当时的意义”①。

但是，汉字经过几千年的发展，有的字本义在今天已经不太明晰，有的字在本义的基础上产生了引申义，有的字本义并非是现在的常用义。在上文我们通过计算也得出148个独体字中有48%是“不透明字”，无法通过回溯字形与现代常用义建立联系。

因此，在解释字义时，我们从实际出发，并不仅仅局限于本义。对于“透明字”我们就解释其本义，例如“日”、“月”、“口”等；对于“半透明字”，其字形与字义之间有辗转的联系，但是通常在本义的基础上有所引申，而引申义在现代汉语中较常用，我们就解释从本义到引申义的演变原理，并指出其引申义，例如“长”的本义是“长者”，因为先民有蓄长发的习惯，故头发越长，年龄越长，生存的时间也长，所以

① 裘锡圭．文字学概要．北京：商务印书馆，2010．142．

“长”后来引申为“长久”之义；对于“不透明字”，即本义与现代常用义相差很远的字，我们在解释本义的同时，更着重指出现在的常用义以提醒学生记住，例如“而”的本义是“人下巴上的胡须”，现在通常用作连词，“又”的本义是“人的手”，现在通常当副词用，表示“再、还”。

第二节　英语解释

《识字卡》针对的是“非汉字文化圈”初学者，但是正因为他们的身份是“非汉字文化圈”的“初学者”，所以识字量必定较少甚至为零。如果《识字卡》不配上相应的英语翻译，对于他们来说，看都无法看懂更谈不上学习汉字了。

目前我们有很多的汉字教材，但是从留学生实际出发配上外语翻译的并不多。有的编写者也考虑到这一问题，在这方面做了一些尝试，如陈火平编写的《趣味汉字》、张惠芬编写的《张老师教汉字·汉字识写课本》。陈火平是新加坡人，英语翻译地道流畅，但是他对汉字的解释却存在很多缺陷甚至有些是错误的。汉字本身解释错误，英语翻译得再好，也只会误导更多的学习者，产生更坏的影响。张惠芬的英语翻译，则十分简短，仅仅对字形和字义作了粗略解释。

本《识字卡》大概分为五部分：图片—字形展示、字义阐释、笔画顺序、词汇例句及小提示。每一部分我们都配上了英语解释，力求做到精练又周到，以方便“非汉字文化圈”初学者学习。在英语翻译方面，可能还有些欠缺、不够地道，但对于每个汉字字形、字义的解释，则进行了科学的分析，尽量避免误导学习者。

第五章 甲乙两级，词汇三千

目前“非汉字文化圈”学生学习汉字的一大特点是：只会认读，不会书写。而且在他们的语言背景中，没有“字”的概念，只有“词”的概念，这种特点迁移到汉语学习中就体现为：关注词汇，忽视汉字。

本《识字卡》的目的是方便“非汉字文化圈”初学者掌握汉字，但是需要指出的是不管是哪个阶段的汉字学习者，学习汉字的最终目标不是掌握汉字的构型系统或理解每个字的来源，而是通过认读汉字理解文章，通过书写汉字表达自己的思想，从而达到交际的目的。所以，我们必须把汉字教学与词汇、语法等结合，实行“语文并进”的策略。

所以，在汉字教学中，我们既要利用汉字理据性强的特点或者利用字源分析，来帮助学生更快掌握汉字，同时也要尊重他们的学习特点，尊重第二语言的习得规律，将汉字与词汇、语法教学结合起来，也只有这样才能从根本上解决“汉字难学”的问题。

因此，在《识字卡》的每个字下面，都列出了由该字组成的词汇。这些词汇包括《汉语水平词汇与汉字等级大纲》（以下简称《词汇与汉字大纲》）中由该字所组成的所有甲级词和乙级词。该大纲共收录了 8 822 个词，按照使用频率分为甲、乙、丙、丁四个等级。其中，甲级词 1 033 个，乙级词 2 018 个，共 3 051 个。“这是多数人经过几十年教学与多种语料反复统计、实践后，得出的第一个词汇量共识”，“同时，根据较大规模的一般语料的词频统计资料，3 000 常用词的覆盖面为 86%”[①]。也就是说甲、乙两级词汇是经过实践和科学统计得出的常用词汇，它覆盖了我们大部分的语言使用情况，初级阶段留学生需要掌握的词汇量就是这 3 000 个常用词。

《识字卡》在词汇问题的处理上，有以下四个特点：第一，甲、乙两级词汇优先列出，将甲级词置于《识字卡》之左，乙级词置于《识字卡》之右；第二，若某字无对应甲、乙两级词汇，则丙、丁级词汇补上，丙级词置于《识字卡》之左，丁级词

---

① 刘英林，宋绍周．论汉语教学字词的统计与分级．汉语水平词汇与汉字等级大纲．北京：经济科学出版社，2001．19．

置于《识字卡》之右；第三，为了方便留学生认读，《识字卡》中的每个词汇都列出了拼音；第四，如果该字所构成的词汇较少，只有一到两个，不能很好地体现在实际口语交流中的用法，则给出一到两个例句，通过例句让学习者更好地理解其用法。

第六章　八百文字，互相参见

第一节　列出字族　增加提示

汉字按照字形结构，分为独体字与合体字。800 个甲级字中，除了《识字卡》中的 148 个独体字，还有 652 个合体字。优先学习独体字，是为了为合体字的学习打下基础。因为在常用汉字中，独体字毕竟占少数，而多数是合体字。汉字按照造字方法，又分为象形字、指事字、会意字、形声字等，合体字中又有很大一部分属于形声字，现代汉字中形声字占到绝大部分。形声字由声旁和形旁构成，很多独体字作为部件参与构成了形声字，在这些形声字中充当声符或意符。我们在第一章第三节已经统计出的 148 个独体字中有 128 个独体字是常用部件，也就是说它们不仅能够独立成字还可作为部件构成大量合体字。在这 148 个独体字中，就有 76 个作为意符或声符参与了 652 个合体字中 319 个的构成。

例如，“女”作为形旁构成了一批形声字“姑、姐、妈、妹、奶、娘、她、姓”，并且在这些字中起表意作用，均表示“女性”义，我们就把这一系列字称为由“女”所构成的字族；又如“元”作为声旁构成了“园、远、院”等字，虽然这四字的声调有差别，但声母、韵母相同，显然“元”有提示语音的作用。

于是，我们把由某个独体字作为构字部件构成的一系列合体字列出来，按照独体字在该合体字中充当的成分，分为“以～为意符的字”和“以～为声符的字”两类。“以～为意符的字”指的是文字学意义上的归类，而非检索学的归类。这样做的目的是“在学生头脑中建立起‘意符’的概念，为文字的识记及词汇的理解打下良好的基础”①。如上面提到的“姑、姐、妈、妹、奶、娘、她、姓”，就列在“以女为意符的字”下面；“以～为声符的字”则是为了在学生头脑中建立起“声符”的概念，如“园、远、院”等字，就列在“以元为声符的字”下面。这样《识字卡》中汉字的学

---

① 曹兆兰.《外国人识字卡》编写探索. 第十届双语双方言研讨会论文选集. 深圳：深圳报业集团出版社，2011. 23.

习就不仅仅局限于148个独体字，而是包括了800甲级字中其他的合体字。

但并不是148个独体字都参与了剩下652个合体字的构成，有的独体字下面既没有“以~为意符的字”，也没有“以~为声符的字”，有的只有其中一项。对于这种情况，《识字卡》设计了一个“小提示”栏目，提示的内容主要有以下几类：①关于该字的笔画、笔顺和字形，如“老”的“小提示”是：“老”的第四笔撇与第三横相交，第五笔短撇与末笔竖弯钩相接；下面是“匕”，不是“七”。②关于该字的繁简字体，如“须”的“小提示”是：“须”的繁体字字形写作“須”。③关于该字读音，如“乐”的小提示是：“乐”有两种读音，作名词指音乐、乐器时，读“yuè”；作形容词指快乐、欢乐时，读“lè”。④关于该字的本义和现代常用义，如“页”的小提示是：现代汉语中，“页”经常用作量词，如“一页纸”、“几页书”，跟“页”的本义无关，是用来记音。⑤关于该字作为构字部件的表意情况，如“目”的小提示是：由“目”组成的汉字，一般与眼睛或眼睛做出的动作有关。

第二节　关于意符或声符的位置问题

在古汉字中，很多字特别是形声字的偏旁位置是不固定的。这一现象在甲骨文、金文时期比较突出，在小篆、隶书时期慢慢减少，到了成熟的楷书时期，情况有了很大的改变，形声字意符和声符不固定的情况虽然还有，但已经很少了。

裘锡圭在《文字学概要》中，列出了形旁和声旁配置的八种类型，也就是我们说的意符和声符的位置问题：左形右声；右形左声；上形下声；下形上声；声占一角；形占一角；形外声内；声外形内。

我们对76个独体字在319个合体字中充当意符或声符的所处位置也做了分类，其中有48个在280个合体字中充当意符，有28个在39个合体字中充当声符。意符的位置有以下九种类型，比裘锡圭的分类多一种，主要是因为我们对“形占一角”的情况进行了细分，分类如下：意符在左、意符在右、意符在上、意符在下、意符在内、意符在外、意符在左上角、意符在右上角、意符在右下角。在我们统计的合体字中，意符在左和在下的情况较多。但有的意符出现的位置类型非常多样，例如“日”作为意符，它的位置就有八种情况：意符在左，有“明、暖、时、晴、晚、昨”；意符在左上角，有“照、题、影”；意符在右，有“旧”；意符在右上角，有“但、提”；意符在右下角，有“借”；意符在上，有“早、是、晨、星”；意符在内，有“宴、间、简、朝”；意符在下，有“春”。

声符的位置主要在右，但也有其他情况，细分起来也有八种类型：声符在右、声符在左、声符在上、声符在下、声符在内、声符在右上角、声符在右下角、声符在中间。其中，在中间和在左都是个例，声符在左的字只有“政”，在中间的字只有“漱”。

根据以上的统计分类，可以看出，这些独体字在合体字充当意符的情况比充当声符的情况多，也就是它们主要还是起提示字义的作用，提示字音的作用有限。同时，意符和声符在合体字中的位置，主要是意符在左、声符在右。这也符合我们经常说到的“左形右声”的情况。但是，意符和声符的位置具有多种类型，我们有必要在《识字卡》中按照上述分类分别列出，以免学生在学习时产生困惑，不知所以。

第三节　关于独体字充当意符或声符后的变形问题

除了上面提到的独体字作为意符或声符在合体字中所处的位置问题，还需注意独体字在充当意符或声符后字形变化的问题。

我们把独体字充当意符或声符后的变形情况分为三种：无变化；有细微变化；有较大变化。“无变化”是指独体字在充当意符或声符后，独体字的字形、笔画都没有任何改变。“有细微变化”是指笔画有改变，例如“火”作为偏旁后，最后一笔捺变为点，“车”作为偏旁后，第三笔横变为提；或者字形虽然有变化，但是仍然能看出原来的形体，例如“雨”作为偏旁后，写成雨字头。“有较大变化”是指字形发生较大变化，已经难以看出原来的形体，例如“刀”作为意符，在“刮、划、刻、利”中写成“刂”；“火”作为意符，在“黑、然、热、熟、照”中写成“灬”；“人”作为意符，在“你、任、什、使、他”等字中写成“亻”；“水”作为意符，在“海、河、湖、江、酒、渴、流”等字中写成“氵”；“衣”作为意符，在“被、袜、初”写成“衤”；“足”作为意符，在“践、路、跑、踢、跳、跟”中写成“⻊”。

在第三章第二节里，我们谈到了汉字的演化情况及趋势。小篆字形复杂、笔画圆转，隶书字形简化、笔画方折。上面提到的“火”作为意符写成“灬”，“人”作为意符写成“亻”，“水”作为意符写成“氵”，“足”作为意符写成“⻊”，都是隶书字形并一直沿用至今。从隶书到楷书的演化过程中，字形也发生了一些变化，上面提到的“刀”作为意符写成“刂”，“衣”作为意符写成“衤”，都是在楷化的过程中出现的，并一直沿用下来。

以上三种不同的情况，《识字卡》做出了不同的处理。对于“无变化”的情况，则无须说明；对于“有细微变化”的情况，则需指出细微变化在哪里，提醒学习者注意；对于“有较大变化”的情况，则需特别说明为何产生这种变化，以免学习者产生误解。

同时，通过对比考察发现，独体字充当意符时，字形产生变化的情况较多。而充当声符时，仅有“正”作为“政”的声符时，有细微变化，其余的都没有发生变化。

第七章　具体问题，具体分析

《识字卡》的编写主要按照以上六点原则进行，但是这六点也并非尽善尽美，在实际操作过程中，也有很多特殊情况不能包括在内。所以，我们对这些特殊情况进行了特殊处理，下面进行详细说明。

第一节　关于繁简字形的处理

新中国成立以来，为了扫除文盲，让更多的人会识字、写字，政府一直致力于汉字的简化运动。1956 年，国务院公布了《汉字简化方案》。经过几年的实践，又于 1964 年总结出《简化字总表》，共制定了 2 235 个简化字。自此，简化字成为中国大陆地区的标准字体，在出版印刷、汉字教学、日常使用等各方面，得到了大力推行。但是目前在中国的香港、澳门和台湾地区，繁体字仍然是通行字体。国外的某些华文学校，在教学中也还是使用繁体字。

《识字卡》的目的是教会留学生认识标准汉字，也就是简体字。虽然大多数“非汉字文化圈”留学生最先学习的是简化字，但是也不排除某些人最初接触的是繁体字。而字体的不统一必定会造成学习、理解和沟通上的误差。另外，虽然在提高全民族文化水平、素质等方面，简体字起了不可忽视的作用，但是从文字学角度来说，繁体字则更能体现古人造字之初的心理思维，承载了更多的传统文化。

在《识字卡》选取的 148 个独体字中，共有 26 个字的繁简字形不同。对于这 26 个字，《识字卡》做了两种不同方式的处理。有些字的繁体字与甲骨文、金文、小篆等一脉相承，如果列出繁体字字形，则能更好地展示该字的发展演变过程，方便学习者理解，避免由古文字到简体字中间出现断层。对于这类字，如“亲（親）”、“见（見）”、“声（聲）”等，我们在字形栏目给出其繁体字，与甲骨文、金文、小篆、楷书简体并列。有些字的繁体字是在后来的发展阶段添加部件而发生繁化的，与甲骨文、金文相去甚远，其简体字反而与古文字字形更一致。对于这类字，如“气（氣）”、“云（雲）”、“电（電）”等，我们不在字形栏目给出繁体字，而是在“小提示”栏目中作出说明。例如“云”，首先说明“云”的繁体字字形是“雲”，再指出以“云”代替“雲”是恢复最初的古文字字形。做出这种处理，是考虑到《识字卡》的教学主要以简化字为标准字体，目的在于学习简化字。

第二节　关于多音字的处理

在现代汉语中，由于汉字繁体与简体、口语与书面语、方言与普通话等并非完全一一对应，因此产生了不少多音字。多音字是指一个字形在现代汉语字典或词典中对应两个或两个以上读音的字。

在《识字卡》选取的148个独体字中，有27个多音字，它们有两个或两个以上的读音。对于多音字，读音有时起区别词性和词义的作用，有时起区别用法的作用，有时起区别语体的作用，有时表示人名、地名等特殊用法，在不同的情况下，读音不同。所以，多音字也是汉字学习的一个难点。

如何处理这27个多音字，《识字卡》主要在以下几个方面进行了尝试：①对于常用多音字，在楷书字形旁边列出每个读音，然后在“小提示”栏目中说明何种情况使用何种读音。例如，“乐（lè/yuè）”，小提示：“乐”作名词指音乐、乐器时，读“yuè”；作形容词指快乐、欢乐时，读“lè”。②对于常用多音字的不常用读音，则不在楷书字形旁标出，并且不作说明。例如，“行”有四个读音：“háng”、“hàng”、“héng”、“xíng”，其中“hàng”和“héng”不常用则不标出，以免加重学生的学习负担，只标出较常用的“háng”和“xíng”，并在“小提示”中进行说明。③对于不常用的多音字，则不标出特殊读音，而只标出其常用读音。如“术（shù/zhú）”、“合（hé/gě）”、“南（nán/ná）”、“其（qí/jī）”、“万（wàn/mò）”、“六（liù/lù）”六个字，第一个读音都是常用读音，第二个读音都是表示中药名、人名、地名等特殊名称时才用，且都只有这一种使用情况。那么《识字卡》就只标出其常用读音，这样一是为了减轻学生的学习负担，二是避免造成学习时出现读音混乱的情况，三是对于初级阶段学生来说，这些非常用读音很少使用，并不需要马上掌握。

第三节　关于特殊字形的处理

经过几千年的发展，某些汉字也发生了较大变化，产生了诸如古今字、异体字、简化字等错综复杂的情况。古今字是从时间方面说的，“一个词的不同书写形式，通行时间往往有前有后。在前者就是在后者的古字，在后者就是在前者的今字”①，例如“求”和“裘”，“裘”就是“求”的今字；异体字是从字形方面说的，指音义相同但字形不同的字，例如在表示脸部时，“靣”和“面”是异体字；简化字是相对于繁体字来说的，一般指的是1956年国务院公布的《汉字简化方案》中的字，例如“长”是“長”的简化字。

《识字卡》希望展示每个字的演变情况，用古代字形来提示现代字义，帮助留学生更快地掌握汉字。但是，并不是每个汉字的古代字形与现代字义都有一脉相承的关系，也有许多特殊情况存在，如古今字、异体字等的出现。对此，我们有必要进行解释，以免给学习者造成困惑和误解。

对于“面”字，因为“靣”已很少使用，为避免加重学习者负担，在《识字卡》中不提及。

对于“长”字，我们也在“小提示”中说明：“长”的繁体字字形是“長”，通过“草书楷化”的方式，对“長”进行了简化。

第四节　关于词汇的处理

在给出甲、乙两级词汇的部分，也出现了一些特殊情况。有的字所组成的词甲级词汇中没有出现，有的乙级词汇中没有出现。例如，由“白”组成的词，甲级词汇中没有，只有乙级词汇中出现了“白菜”和“白天”两个词。在词汇部分，只列两个词组，远远不能很好地体现这个字的用法。因此，对于这种只有甲级词或只有乙级词的情况，《识字卡》将词汇放在左边，然后在右边给出相应的例句，让学生在实际语境和使用中，体会该字、该词的用法。所以，我们按照以下的方法来处理“白”这个字：

① 裘锡圭. 文字学概要. 北京：商务印书馆，2010. 270.

白菜 báicài Chinese cabbage 白天 báitiān daytime	我喜欢吃白菜。 Wǒ xǐhuān chī báicài. I like eating Chinese cabbage 你白天在干什么？ Nǐ báitiān zài gàn shénme? What do you do during daytime?

有的字所组成的词甲、乙两级词汇都没有。对于这种情况，我们不局限于甲、乙级词汇，而是将词汇范围扩大到丙级、丁级。例如“角”，将丙级词汇“角度”、“角落”置于《识字卡》左边，丁级词汇“三角”置于右边。

有的字在甲、乙、丙、丁四级词汇中都没有相应的词组出现。对于这种情况，《识字卡》就给出该字在实际使用中所组成的词汇。例如，“页”在实际使用中，通常有两种用法：一是指纸张，如“活页”、“页码”等；二是作量词，一般用来修饰纸，如“一页纸”、“几页书”等。那么，我们就把这些相关的词汇列出来。

有的字所组成的词汇，由于社会政治、经济的发展变化，该词所代表的实际事物已经消失，而《词汇与汉字大纲》由于具有一定的滞后性，仍然列出该词。对于这种情况，《识字卡》果断地将其删去。例如“马”，在甲级词汇中有“马克”一词，但由于欧元的使用，“马克”早已退出历史舞台，该词汇在实际口语交流中已不属于常用词。

还有一种情况是，某些字所组成的词汇特别多，也很常用，但是《识字卡》的篇幅有限，不能完全列举出来。例如，由“面”组成的乙级词汇多达 20 个，像“东面”、“西面”、“南面”、“北面”这些用法完全相同的词汇，从篇幅考虑就删掉了其中的“西面”和“北面”。

总之，在词汇处理中，《识字卡》尽量列出全部甲级词和乙级词，并且控制在一定数量以内。对于没有甲、乙级词汇的字，我们则补充添加其在实际使用的词汇。对于甲、乙级词汇过多，超过一定篇幅的字，我们则有选择地删除其所组成的词汇。

第五节 关于“以～为声符的字”的处理

列出“以～为声符的字”，是为了在独体字的基础上，让学习者在头脑中建立起“字族”的概念，以一个独体字的学习带动一串合体字的学习。为了达到这种效果，必须筛选出与该独体字联系最紧密、最自然并以其为声符的一系列合体字。所以，《识字卡》只列出与该独体字声母、韵母均相同的合体字。例如，以“方”为声符的字有“房”、“访”、“放”。

对于音近字、只有声母相同或只有韵母相同的字，则不列出，例如“果”的音近字“棵”、“课”，不列出。由于语音的发展变化，在某一阶段，曾以该独体字为声符，但是在现代汉语中的读音则与之不同的字，也不列出，例如，“技”在《说文解字》中是“从手，支声”。但是，在现代汉语中，“技”虽然有“支”这一部件，但是两者声母不同，读音之间的联系不够紧密。如果列出，不但无助于学习，反而会带来干扰、造成迷惑。

第六节　关于古代文化传播与现代汉字教学的处理

古代汉字承载着中国传统文化，现代汉字作为语言的交流沟通工具仍在广泛使用。那么《识字卡》的目的到底在于传播古代文化，还是侧重现代汉字的教学呢？我们认为，传播古代文化与现代汉字的教学，两者之间并不矛盾。关键问题在于如何处理两者之间的关系。如果处理好了两者关系，那么传播古代文化将会促进现代汉字的学习，学习现代汉字也有助于了解古代文化，它们之间就会形成相互促进、和谐统一的关系。

在字形展示部分，《识字卡》列出了甲骨文、金文、小篆、隶书等古代字形，有助于学习者了解汉字文化，激发他们的学习兴趣。同时，这些字形一方面展示了从古代汉字到现代简化字的过程，另一方面字形能够显示字义，有助于现代汉字的学习。

在词汇和“小提示”部分，《识字卡》则更注重现代汉字的教学。词汇部分列出了该字所组成的常用词以及一些例句，侧重于讲解该字在语言交流中的使用情况。“小提示”部分则从笔画字形、繁简字体、读音、字义等方面，对该字在现代汉语中的实际应用作了补充说明。

在字义解释部分，《识字卡》则将古代文化传播与现代汉字教学进行了结合。首先根据字形解释本义、展示演变，再给出引申义或现代常用义。例如“尤”，首先解释“在甲骨文和金文中，‘[illegible]’是手臂形，上有一斜画像是手臂上长了某种东西，用斜画标明，所以‘尤’的本义指‘肉瘤’”，再阐述“古人认为长在手臂的瘤是不正常的，‘尤’又引申有‘特别、特异’之义”，接着说明“现在‘尤’通常用作副词，表示‘尤其、特别’之义”。这样，学习者不仅了解了古人造“尤”时的思维特点，还明白了它的现代用法。

第七节　关于某些术语的处理

形声字是汉字的基本造字方法之一，现在也通常指由形符和声符两部分组成的一类汉字，例如“脸”、“路”、“字”、“政”、“住”等字。在《识字卡》中，我们主要讲解独体字，但是这些独体字往往构成了一大批形声字，或者说是一大批形声字的构成部件。这些独体字或充当形声字的意符或充当声符。例如，“月”是“脸”的意符，“足”是“路”的意符，“子”是“字”的声符，“正”是“政”的声符，“主”是“住”的声符。这一系列形声字都列在了《识字卡》的下方。为了避免初学者理解形声字的困难，也为了明确指出某个独体字在一批形声字中表音还是表意，它们没有被称为“形声字”，而是被称为“以～为意符的字”或“以～为声符的字”。例如“脸”称为“以‘月’为意符的字”，“字”称为“以‘子’为声符的字”。因此，在《识字卡》中，所有的形声字都被分为两类，一是“以～为意符的字”，二是“以～为声符的字”。

赵诚先生在《甲骨文字学纲要》中认为甲骨文“在本质上是表音的，但有比较突出的以形表意的特征”①，因此不宜把以音表意的字称为假借字，所以在他的一些著作如《甲骨文简明词典》中，他将假借字称为借音字或记音字。在本文中，我们不讨论甲骨文或汉字究竟是表音文字还是表意文字或是意音文字，只是采用赵诚先生的术语称谓，将“假借字”称为“记音字”，以表明这种字的字形与字义并无联系，主要是用来记录字音的，以方便汉字初学者理解，而不必大费周折解释什么是“假借字”。

---

① 赵诚．甲骨文字学纲要．北京：中华书局，2005．50．

参考文献

[1] 国家汉语水平考试委员会办公室考试中心. 汉语水平词汇与汉字等级大纲. 北京：经济科学出版社，2001.

[2] 中华人民共和国教育部国家语言文字工作委员会. 现代常用独体字规范. 北京：语文出版社，2009.

[3] 段玉裁. 说文解字注. 郑州：中州古籍出版社，2006.

[4] 汉语大字典编辑委员会. 汉语大字典. 武汉：湖北辞书出版社，成都：四川辞书出版社，1986.

[5] 陈梦家. 中国文字学. 北京：中华书局，2006.

[6] 裘锡圭. 文字学概要. 北京：商务印书馆，2010.

[7] 赵诚. 甲骨文字学纲要. 北京：中华书局，2005.

[8] 曹兆兰. 金文与殷周女性文化. 北京：北京大学出版社，2004.

[9] [日] 白川静. 金文通释选译. 曹兆兰选译. 武汉：武汉大学出版社，2000.

[10] 邹晓丽. 基础汉字形义释源：《说文》部首今读本义. 北京：中华书局，2007.

[11] 左民安. 细说汉字——1 000 个汉字的起源与演变. 北京：九州出版社，2005.

[12] 熊国英. 图释古汉字. 济南：齐鲁书社，2006.

[13] 郑振峰等. 汉字学. 北京：语文出版社，2005.

[14] 吕必松. 汉语和汉语作为第二语言教学. 北京：北京大学出版社，2007.

[15] 周健. 汉字教学理论与方法. 北京：北京大学出版社，2007.

[16] 徐彩华. 汉字认知与汉字学习心理研究. 北京：知识产权出版社，2010.

[17] 顾安达，江新，万业馨. 汉字的认知与教学：西方学习者汉字认知国际研讨会论文集. 北京：北京语言大学出版社，2007.

[18] 佟大汶. 图解汉字. 西安：三秦出版社，2004.

[19] 韩鉴堂. 汉字文化图说. 北京：北京语言大学出版社，2005.

[20] 周健. 汉字突破. 北京：北京大学出版社，2005.

[21] 施正宇. 新编汉字津梁. 北京：北京大学出版社，2005.

[22] 易洪川. 阶梯汉语·初级汉字. 北京：华语教学出版社，2006.

[23] 张惠芬. 张老师教汉字·汉字识写课本. 北京：北京语言大学出版社，2005.

[24] 张旺熹. 从汉字部件到汉字结构——谈对外汉字教学. 世界汉语教学，1990（2）.

[25] 李大遂. 对外汉字教学发展与研究概述. 暨南大学华文学院学报，2004（2）.

[26] 钱学烈. 对外汉字教学实验报告. 北京大学学报（哲学社会科学版），1998（3）.

[27] 尤浩杰. 笔画数、部件数和拓扑结构类型对非汉字文化圈学习者汉字掌握的影响. 世界汉语教学，2003（2）.

[28] 石定果，万业馨. 关于对外汉字教学的调查报告. 语言教学与研究，1998（1）.

[29] 石定果. 汉字研究与对外汉语教学. 语言教学与研究，1997（1）.

[30] 柳燕梅，江新. 欧美学生汉字学习方法的实验研究. 世界汉语教学——回忆默写法与重复抄写法的比较，2003（1）.

[31] 高明. 中国古文字学通论. 北京：北京大学出版社，1996.

[32] 苏培成. 现代汉字学纲要. 北京：北京大学出版社，2001.

[33] 张和生. 基于二语教学的汉字构形理据量化研究. 北京师范大学学报（社会科学版），2011（6）.